Finding Fawna
Using Cancer for Awakening

By Fawna Bews version 2006 and
Fawna Bews version 2013

Cover Photo by Janet Hughes Pliszka
Visual Hues Photography
www.visualhues.com

ISBN **1535251301**

© 2013 by Fawna Bews Edition 1

All rights reserved. Copyright under Berne Copyright Convention, Universal Copyright Convention, and Pan-American Copyright Convention. No part of this book may be reproduced, stored in a retrieval system, or transmitted in any form, or by any means, electronic, mechanical, photocopying, recording or otherwise, without prior permission of the author.

To my husband Dusty and
My parents Ross and Gail Edey;
The perfect balance.

Introduction

Thank You for taking the time to read this story. There are few people who have not felt the punishing impact of cancer. The word cancer has developed a powerful presence in our society, and as the years go by the treatment of cancer seem to carry the same weight of dread as the diagnosis itself.
Every experience is unique, I offer this story as a 'happy ending' alternative to how this story often goes. From this vantage point it is about so much more than cancer.
I wondered for years why the book I finished in 2006 was not moving out of my computer. It makes more sense now as I finish a second journey with cancer and feel ready to truly put this story out into the world and the experience of cancer behind me.
A couple of things have become clear to me, that any event has an external and an internal 'reality' to it and that nothing happens to us in isolation. We are truly in this together.
On a practical note, what you are about to read is the story of diagnosis, treatment and recovery from cancer beginning in 2000 and finishing in 2012. This is a compilation of reflections, journalling (the funky font) and blogging.
The process of journaling and blogging and now sharing this story has been healing for me. In this story perhaps you will find pieces of yourself.

Journey One

Chapter One
"It doesn't look good, Sweetie"

The year 2000; fear hovered in the air as we switched over the millennium. Prophecies of the end of the world, threats of computers crashing, as the year slipped in without a problem, my part in the collective sigh was short lived.

A 28 year old mother of 2 toddlers, I had just finished a Master's Degree in Counseling and was feeling like I had things under control. In retrospect, 'in control' was a strong driver in my life until this point, and a complete delusion.

After visiting the doctor on three different occasions for vague symptoms: nagging cough, headaches, 'pressure' and what I thought was a fatter neck, I found myself in the office again. This doctor, who had brought me through two pregnancies, and I chatted easily and when I mentioned that I felt that I may have lost weight she marched me down to the scale. I had gone down a few pounds but what caught her attention was my labored breathing when we returned from our short walk.

"Have you noticed that you are short of breath?" she questioned.

Honestly I hadn't noticed. I believe this symptom came on so slowly that I had adapted, either that or I was just completely disconnected from my body. She didn't look terribly concerned but decided that we had better have a chest x-ray.

I drove up to our small hospital and sitting in the darkened room I could see the technician through the glass, I noticed that she was looking at my films and talking on the phone. A small warning bell went off in my mind, 'bing'. She instructed me that I was to take the x-rays with me to show Dr. Lumby the next day.

Once they were in my hot little hands I was quick to pour over them, I was incredibly relieved to see nothing strange in my head, and not sure what exactly was going on in my chest. I didn't think it looked just right but I wasn't too concerned. My background in Physical Therapy gave me a good idea of how to read an x-ray but I had mostly looked at bones.

I went to bed not knowing that the next morning my life would change.

The next day I had a chiropractic appointment before seeing my doctor, I'd never been to the chiropractor but I'd had a nagging pain in my back that acupuncture wasn't quite getting. He and I looked at the films and he too remarked on the 'fuzzy' chest. We had a long discussion and we ran out of time for an actual adjustment, I promised to come back afterwards and I took my pictures across the street where my doctor was waiting. She was looking troubled and was quick to grab the films and put them up on the screen.

"It doesn't look good sweetie"

These words would become burned into my mind. She explained that it was most likely a Hodgkin's Lymphoma and expounded on the good treatment alternatives, trying to make it light. She had been my doctor for 5 years and her concern was genuine, her distress obvious.

In shock, I drove directly to my husband, laid my head on his chest and told him, "I might have Hodgkin's Disease." I believe that he answered, "What does that mean?" It would be a few days before I uttered the 'C' word and even longer for him.

Let me back up a little. In September of 1999 I started to notice a pressure in my head when I bent down to do up the kid's jackets. Jake was 2 and Paige was 18 months old, they required much crouching. After getting them in their car seats I was starting to sit a moment and rest, I now realize I was catching my breath. My other symptoms, fatigue and a persistent cough were easily explained away. I had just finished a Master's degree and had not had a full night's sleep in over 2 years.

I did however seek medical attention and each time was told, "There are many virus's going around."

Christmas came and went and I hated all the pictures. I really thought my neck looked fat, or weird, or something.

For New Years that year my parents took the kids and Dusty and I went on a ski trip. I got out of bed and got dressed to go out once-ONCE! This was very unusual, I love to ski, and I like to go out for dinner even more. I spent the holiday lying in bed slathered in Vicks Vapo-Rub watching Court TV. My cough was nagging and I was intensely paranoid about driving, keeping my eyes closed for most of the drive down to Montana and back.

Over this time I sought relief from complementary medicine and found some decrease in the symptoms with acupuncture.

I began to think that my neck was getting wider and that my neck veins seemed to be sticking out, I was mildly alarmed, a doctor assured me that I was just 'lean'. At 5'4 and 150 lbs. I wasn't really lean, but I bought it.

After we stood still a few moments, neither of us sure what to do, Dusty joined me to go and get the kids. My brother Joel was watching them at our workplace, the Stampede Ranch for Kids. We shared the news and Joel, Dusty and I were shell shocked quiet. We sat at my parent's old round table, each of us staring into space.

I made the decision not to tell my parents, who were in Mexico, until I knew more. My Aunt, who also worked with us, quickly overturned this decision "bullshit, you get on that phone right now or I will." The phone call was quick and I tried to be casual.

Somewhere in this time I entered la-la land and busied myself with care and attention to the babies. I told some friends, downplaying any seriousness or concerns.

My doctor called the next day, having gotten me in to see a specialist in 3 days. So much for wait times in the Canadian health care system! I phoned to tell Mom and Dad and couldn't get a hold of them; they were already half way home.

I went to the first specialist on my own. After sitting in his waiting room for over an hour he quickly determined that he wouldn't be able to biopsy and I was going to need a thoracic surgeon. Two days later I saw my second surgeon.

Unfortunately when my parents arrived home they consulted the medical books on their shelves (dated 1963). Apparently, the prognosis for lymphoma in the 60's was very, very bad. My mom, now completely freaked out, was with me to see the next specialist.

By this time I had also had a CT scan, the speed of all of this should have been a clue to me that this was serious, but as I said, I was in la-la land.

The surgeon surveyed the scan and noted that there was a 10 by 12 cm tumor in my chest with metastases to my lungs and pancreas. Due to my age there was still an assumption that it was Hodgkin's disease; surgery would be necessary to know for sure.

After only a few minutes he said, "I want you in the hospital for this biopsy. I calmly told him "Sorry, I can't; I have little kids, I'll get organized and maybe do a day surgery.

My Mom will never forgive him for starting to cry. He insisted "No, I need you to walk across the parking lot and admit yourself into Emergency-I need you in there right now"

My Mom and I contained ourselves, denial is a grand thing. We walked across the parking lot, sat for hours, watching the strange sea of humanity that fills an emergency room and finally I was admitted to a temporary little room. It may have been a repurposed broom closet. The room was bright, stark and I was heartsick to be away from the kids.

The next day I was admitted to the heart ward. I was younger than the other residents by 40 years and still remarkably healthy. This is really where this adventure began. Like any epic adventure there were two parts, the outside saga and the inner drama. I hope to capture both-a lot of what was to happen inside heavily influenced how I experienced what was happening to me and at times the inner and outer worlds were in stark contrast to one another. This realization of the influence of the inside on the outside and not always the other way around has had a profound effect and has shifted by life.

I was reflective and in horror that I had to be in there for "5 or 6 days-little did I know the extent of hospitalization that would be required. The size of the tumor was considerable and I found myself focused on this for a bit. I think that this may be the time when Grace began to take my hand. Over the course of the next few months I would be given comforting messages or mantras that would keep me relatively calm and peaceful. This first one was:

"The tumor is big, but I am bigger"

Helping me to re-focus on all the parts of me that were healthy, my spirit and my family and my life and the better part of the body.

Being alone in the hospital and feeling relatively good was surreal. I would wander the halls, sit in bed and wait for the shower feeling exactly as healthy as I had felt the week before at home. I was a perfect test case for this teaching hospital, doctorate students were sent through regularly, it was not readily obvious what was going on.

That first week was a flurry of tests and doctors- and this would be the story of the next 3 months.

Chapter Two
Attachment vs. Commitment

Then the crying started. My crying was completely about the kids. How could I be away from them? Are they okay? Am I okay? Are they going to forget about me?

> January 28
> I'm afraid the kids will forget me or feel like they've been abandoned by their Mom. I hope so bad that my Mom and Dad bring them up to see me - Tammy is going to see them more this week than I am.
>
> I am sad and afraid - but I know that it is important for me to get better so that I can be a mom in the long run rather than this week.

So, here I was, 28 years old in a big room with 3 senior citizens. All three were confined to bed, two had just had open-heart surgery and one spent her awake time trying to get out of bed despite doctors' orders to stay put. The entire floor was so immobile that I nearly gave a nurse a heart attack when I got up to notify someone about my escape artist roommate.

I was to be there for a week to have a biopsy. The biopsy would require opening my chest and taking a piece of the tumor out, unfortunately with a lymphoma it was not possible to take it all out, messing with it can just make it spread. This tumor was situated in an area that made it dangerous for me to be put out completely. All procedures would be done under local anesthesia.

It was around this time when I realized how difficult breathing was. Unannounced, as I lay resting in my bed, a physician with 6 students filed into my room. They crowded around and the teaching Physician asked permission for them to question me. He asked them to try to figure out why I was there. They asked their questions and then requested that I lay flat, the physician asked if I had any problems laying flat. "No, no I'm fine" I answered. Within seconds of laying flat my lips were blue and the doctor had me sitting up-watch for this type of stoic patient he lectured the students. I wasn't being stoic, I honestly hadn't noticed and now it made sense why I hadn't been sleeping. Again in hindsight I realize how disconnected I was from my physical body.

None of the students guessed and when he told them what was going on I could see the concern in their eyes-they hadn't developed their doctors shells yet. This made me feel better about the family doctors who had missed the diagnosis before Christmas. The thought of being in hospital for Christmas bothered me a lot so I figured that the timing was perfect and I didn't harbor resentment towards the misdiagnosis. I heard later that the doctors felt terrible about it.

My journal became my solace. I wrote Cancer journal at the top and Dusty said, "Don't do that, he was still avoiding the word. I had been a lifelong journal writer and the information was coming hard and fast, it gave me both something to do and a sense of control in a seemingly out of control situation. I detailed the mundane details, medical information and my innermost feelings.

Having just finished a Masters' degree in counseling it was a chance to 'walk my talk.' Affirmations became a staple:

January 28, 2000

*I will be relaxed and safe during my biopsy. My doctors and their staff are exceptional people who care for me. I will recover quickly and remain strong in receiving and recovering from the treatments that are needed. I will live a long, joyous and people centered life. I will serve a greater purpose.

This is a wonderful adventure and my spirit is more than strong enough to conquer and eliminate this cancer, leaving a well and 'stronger than ever' body
*

I added the stars in my journal because I returned to this one often. After a couple of delays (apparently thoracic surgeons are very busy) I was preparing for surgery. The delays were heart wrenching and I was grieving every minute that I was away from the kids. I cried and lamented to myself, I cursed having to wait for my biopsy, more concerned about getting home than finding out what was going on.

Fortunately a dear friend had given me Naomi Rachel Ramen's book, Kitchen Table Wisdom. This dear book provided me with the turning point, the point at which I believe that I began to heal:

January 29, 2000
Attachment vs. Commitment pg. 192

I am going to choose to be <u>committed</u> to Jake and Paige rather than <u>attached</u>. I am committed to doing what is best for them and the best thing right now is that they stay happy and cared for and that I look after getting back to them ASAP.

Interesting that I'm on a floor of 'broken hearts'

Once I took hold of this commitment I began to fully embrace the idea of getting better. Still eager to get the surgery over with I was overjoyed when the time finally came. Unknown to my family I did a little good-bye letter and very tiny will.

January 30, 2000

Living Will Thoughts

In the event that something happens:

-Resuscitate (of course)

-Life support- 1 month- if brain gone- let me go

-It's okay to put me in an institution if you need to- but please be a thorn in their side.

-I have had a <u>wonderful life</u>- no regrets.

-I know that everything will be <u>OK</u>

-Donate <u>everything</u> you can!!

Fawna Bews

When surgery day came, I was calm. Lying in the waiting area in a bed-on-wheels all alone I could feel the prayers. The sensation was one of floating on clouds. I had an awareness of softness and positivity comforting me. As I lay here, affirmations running through my brain, concentrating on breathing-a woman walked out of surgery with a grapefruit. I just started to laugh, was this their measuring device? They always equate tumors to food "orange sized, walnut sized". I welcomed laughing and hospitals can be seriously funny places.

The actual procedure itself I remember well. Initially they tried to put an I.V. into my foot, I became dizzy, nauseous and just about passed out. Once they were able to find a vein I was heavily medicated, but could feel the pressure of everything. I could hear the scraping of the bone and the discussion between the surgeon and nurses. I was completely aware and had remarkable shooting pains in my back. The surgeon kept saying, "Sorry, sorry, that was me." They opened up two ribs and picked some of the tumor out. I asked them to take it all out, but, as I said before, not an option.

In the recovery room I drifted in and out and a precious moment came upon the room. The man in the bed beside me took to talking and he talked like we were in a beautiful hotel. He was older but flirty and the drug induced mood was light and hazy as we discussed our accommodations, the service and the possibility of meeting at poolside. These little moments of Grace sustained me, after returning to my room I was witness to another:

February 1, 2000

Hermina, one of my roommates, was tucked into bed by her daughter Kate last night in an absolutely beautiful ritual. I was touched by the intimacy and I now see why this very sick woman appears to be recovering. She was tucked in and gently kissed on the face with reverence-it was beautiful.

Aggressive Large B-Cell Tumor Non-Hodgkin's

A cancer usually found in men over 60.

> I started on prednisone-I feel slightly manic-I'm not too sure that my mind is not just protecting itself.
>
> NON HODGKINS LYMPHOMA, LARGE B CELL, FAST GROWING-treatment comes soon.
>
> Love is absolutely streaming in to my room-I'm actually feeling all of these prayers! I'm getting pretty corny!!!
>
> Dusty to dinner and had a pretty good talk with him-I love him SO MUCH, he is my home base.
>
> Started prednisone-ooh-getting a bit repetitive (see manic)
>
> Well, I'm drinking my radioactive drink.
>
> Paul and Beth in while I was out.
>
> Lots of visitors expected tomorrow.
>
> Day Nurse-Shawna
>
> Night-Sheila

Day-Melissa

February 3, 2000, "Another day in this cruel episode of candid camera"

I awoke to drink a full litre of liquefied chalk! And then straight to the CT scan-very nice porter and Steve at Diagnostic Imaging was awesome. CT of chest, abdomen and pelvis.

Nice shower, packed some stuff up in case I move-Believe it or not about 1 hour after hearing there was no room on Unit 57 for me-I'm lying in bed and I hear "Code blue on Unit 57, Code Blue on Unit 57" I thank you God, But I didn't need a bed that badly!!!

I will miss my sweet roommates.

Dawn Purdy from spiritual services was by-when I tried to tell her about all the people praying for me I started to cry. She was going to cry, if I read in a book about someone in the same circumstances I would bawl my head off.

I am pain free today-no pain killers.

I think the prednisone makes me high! My face may be puffy already.

Before there could be a treatment plan there would need to be more tests, in other words, is it worth doing anything?

When they had initially mentioned a bone marrow test I was terrified. In Physical Therapy school I had heard that this was extremely painful. However, as was to become a pattern, it was less terrible than expected.

Instead of going to a different room the intern assigned to me, Dr. Li, showed up with his hand drill and bottles. He was extremely kind and well intentioned and the space felt strangely sacred. I believe it was the first time he had done this on his own, he was in complete concentration and feeling terrible about how long it was taking him-he was covered in sweat by the time he was done. He remarked that 28 year old bones are certainly stronger than older ones! I have tried to google search Dr. Li many times since leaving the hospital without luck. He and I started a friendship that day and he continued to visit me even past his internship.

> February 2, 2010
>
> 2 rounds of MD's in to look at me today-I kind of enjoyed this. Bone Marrow extraction from Dr. Li-thanks to him not very traumatic-a bit of pressure. Apparently my bones are very hard-he was sweating and worked hard to get what he needed. (I'm big boned after all!)
>
> Asked for permission to do an AIDS test-wouldn't that be a kick in the head?!!!

Happily the bone marrow test and AIDS tests were negative.

These first few weeks in the hospital were mind boggling on a few fronts-the reality of the situation balanced with an outpouring of love from my community. In one day I had 21 visitors, my freezer was filled with casseroles and my room looked like a flower shop! So much to be grateful for.

Other People

In the years since my first diagnosis and recovery I have talked with hundreds of other cancer patients. Generally our conversation quickly turns to 'other people.' The spectrum of behaviors in friends and family is drastic and often completely unpredictable. There were those who had become close who remained distant while I was in treatment, those who were 'acquaintances' who were rocks of support. There were those that were bereft and those that helped me with black humor.

My brother Fred for example came in to visit me and opened up his visit with "I would stay longer but I just wasted 20 minutes talking to someone down the hall-all of you cancer patients look the same to me."

There were people who acted as gate keepers and those who came just because they felt guided. One friend, who I had not been particularly close to, came on one of my darker days. She gave me a rosary that was made from the rose petals from her brother's funeral and in one of the precious moments she just sat and stroked my leg while I rested-no words.

I heard from old boyfriends, bus drivers and strangers. I was surprised by some of the people who just couldn't visit. The overriding feeling however was that this was not happening to me alone. This was very much a shared experience.

Chapter 3
Treatment

This diagnosis meant NOT leaving the hospital-total disappointment and lots of refocusing on the commitment vs. attachment message was required.

I no longer needed to be on the Thoracic Unit with my elderly friends, but needed to be on the inpatient cancer floor-my new home away from home, Unit 57.

> February 4, 2000
>
> I've been thinking that there are many things I want to do-ponder, etc. Before I thought there was nothing I had to talk about to a counselor about and now there seems to be lots, maybe if I record some things I will stop perseverating on them.
>
> Things I need to do:
>
> 1. Ask Kim if she will paint my head when it's bald (flowers and vines).
> 2. Make up with Jodi.
> 3. Make up a visualization of the Cancer leaving that works for me. The "you are big but I am bigger works-but I can't seem to visualize where it [the cancer] is going to!! Collapsing in on

itself? Or flying out like in "The Green Mile." I can't quite get the right one.
4. Get in a support group-studies prove you live longer.
5. Stop biting my nails, picking my nose and picking my head-all bad for when I'm immunosuppressed. May release some emotions that I am hiding.
6. I asked to tap into the energy of the healer last night from the past, now and the future and I had the most wonderful feelings from my toes all the way through-felt awesome-I will be doing that again.
7. Maybe I will think of the tumor and it's outbuildings in the lungs and pancreas as my body's way of 'building without a permit'. My heart put a whole second floor on-a party room for all my friends and family and although a good idea-all of this building is not up to code and I am the MD (Municipal District) and I am ordering that all non-permitted building be demolished.

**There is a good chance that this prednisone is making me manic!

Unit 57 is creepily nice. There were some similarities with the Thoracic Unit, it was comparable to moving from the Super 8 to the Hilton!

> This unit is very nice-but very cancery-pamphlets, nice nurses, homier décor-comforting but not. It says, "We know you're really not well so we will be nicer to you over here."

Everyone was super smiley, quiet and kind-even the cleaning staff. There were nicer pictures, nicer furniture, puzzles, games and exercise equipment. All of it said, "Uh, oh-you are in trouble now."

I was informed that my first chemotherapy treatment would be that week.

I know that I had a choice in this, but I honestly did not consider not having the chemo, I was willing to do whatever it took. From day one I had 'visualized' myself as an old woman, I carried this image with me in every decision.

Since this time I have come to know several people who have chosen not to take chemo. It is such a loaded word-instilling fear in the hearts of men' as it were. Coming in with some western medical background I don't think I was as suspicious as some people and have always had a comfort in the hospital setting. I have definitely been more immersed in the natural health care world since then, but at the time I was going to do EVERYTHING it took to come out the other side. I would not however suggest that this is the answer for everyone.

I have a little soapbox when it comes to chemotherapy. They have come so far with the drugs that they have for the side effects, I did not have the same experience that my grandmother had. There may be a conspiracy of the drug companies-I don't know-what I do know is that all I met with were concerned individuals who wanted me to live.

I believe that fear is at least as dangerous as chemotherapy and if you cannot get over believing that it is only poison, then you must consider finding a way to change it at the level of the mind, or reconsider the option.

As it turned out, the tumor was large and aggressive and had metastasized, I was in the position of having a Stage IV cancer, and treatment options of going slow were not offered.

As I have already stated, I started out on prednisone, a steroid.

As an aside, the focus on beauty in our culture is as relevant during cancer treatment as any time. For me it was the prednisone, I did not want a fat face. Facing a life threatening illness and worried about fat face, I smiled at the awareness, the absurdity! I remember my friend Karen going through chemotherapy and about to face mastectomy and hair loss, "I'm losing the best parts of me" she lamented; these were far from the best parts of Karen, who was a celebrated friend and mother. Along the same crazy lines was the reaction to my weight loss, I had many women say, "Well, at least you can wear Shannon's clothes (my slim and beautiful sister in law)." These comments were illuminating on the value that we put on 'skinny'.

What my doctor recommended was a clinical trial. High Dose Chemotherapy with a Stem Cell Rescue. He admitted that this was extremely aggressive treatment but felt that we had passed the opportunity for less invasive measures. My parents, Dusty and I listened to the outline, and I was on board when he said, in response to my "what would you do?", "If you were my sister this is what I would recommend." I know that doctors have to be very careful with what they say, so this was strong doctor talk.

I remember signing many papers and thinking that it suited me just fine, the regular protocol was 9 months, this one was 3-4. Hitting it hard and fast suited my personality; I was still in la-la land.

> Feb 4, 2010-2 weeks after my visit to the doctor and I am having my first chemotherapy treatment. I spent the day deep breathing, doing positive affirmations- really working it. I spent some time patching up a difficulty with a dear friend and when the time came I was peacefully laying in my bed. It seems funny now,

but one of my friends, husbands mothers- that's right-friends husbands mother-came to visit me-right at chemo time. I had never met this woman and she had piles and piles of questions. Picture me forcefully being peaceful, underlain with super irritation, makes me laugh now. She stayed the whole time... So I waited and waited, had my IV, and finally I said to the nurse, "okay-when is the chemotherapy coming? "You've been on it for 30 minutes" I said, "WHAT?!" The clear bag of liquid running quietly into my arm was CHEMO. I had been waiting for the people in lead suits to enter my room with a neon green potion. I had expected to feel something-how anticlimactic. So I settled into finishing chemo. #1 with chatty Cathy, my friends husbands Mom.

My Chemo affirmation:

Today's chemo will be okay-I am relaxed and safe, my doctors and my nurses are exceptional human beings who know what they are doing and care very much about me. I have a thousand prayers to rest and float on.

Chapter 4
Gratitude

We, my family and I, were determined to take every approach available to us. On a 'day pass' we went to visit an oncology acupuncturist. Dr. Xeng had been an oncologist in China. She is a gentle and lovely woman and her husband was her office manager. Her manner was professional and confident and after assessing me she assured me that she could help. She planned to see me until my second chemo, stop and then resume when the transplant was over. My initial treatments were amazing, I felt energized and renewed after each one.

One unintended side effect was that Dr. Xeng told my parents that I was not to get cold. They take instructions seriously and this meant that their vehicle was blasting hot for all of their chauffeuring me around! I would lay panting in the back thinking that this was not what Dr. Xeng had intended.

This takes me back to the beauty of this time. There was an intensity and poignancy in the conversations. When I think of the times going to and from acupuncture, usually involving lunch at a pub, I remember enjoying the intimacy of discussion. With 2 little kids I had spent little to no time with anyone in conversation over the past couple of years, let alone my parents. After acupuncture we would go for lunch and the gravity of the situation led to deep and meaningful conversation. This would be one of the things I would miss when I reentered the land of the 'living' and I never have regained a love of 'small talk', looking to take it deeper whenever possible.

My parents were understandably shaken (understatement)?. I'm sure that this entire event was the most traumatic for them. To be honest, this irritated me for a while, I was trying to stay positive and their anxious energy was distracting, their daily visits seemed unnecessary. Once I sat with it though I was able to see that I would be out of my head if it were Jake or Paige. Not only that but they were the primary caretakers of the kids, still running their business (a group home for kids) and making the effort to see me every day. In retrospect I don't know how they did it.

Here's how I was doing, random…

Feb 6, 2000

I need red pajamas

One profound feeling that I keep having is that I'm disappointed in myself-I read things in these books and I think-I already know this and I still let this happen" I need to remind myself to be kind to myself and maybe I have an even higher purpose than just this.

I'm going to write and write.

RN Delphi-very nice

I really want to spend special time with the kids coming up. I think it is important for them to come in while I'm in here.

I am going to do really, really well. I am going to live a long and healthy life. I am going to learn discipline and joy in keeping house. I have 3-4 months off now (be careful what you wish for)!

Gratitude

I am so lucky to be Canadian and have the opportunity to have this top notch care.

I'm grateful for my young happy roommate

I'm grateful for my Mom and Dad's commitment to the kids and the lack of my need for guilt or worry.

I'm grateful for my Dusty and Kids

I'm grateful for the Residents who have given me their time and true care (Dr. Li and the tall grey haired girl).

Funny...

My Dad accidentally got off the third floor instead of the 5th-it was the locked Alzheimer's floor and he had to do some fast-talking to get 'let out'.

So during this time I saw the acupuncturist and moved back and forth from the hospital to some wonderful friends in the city to home depending on my white blood cell count. The chemo was like having a bad hangover. I was tired and I walked slowly, I became slower and slower as the treatment went on and wished for closer and closer parking spots. My Dad is notorious for taking the furthest away spot and toward the end I would look at that walk across the parking lot as if it were miles across the desert.

My first trip home was after 2 weeks. When I'd left home I'd just been going to the specialist! My house was

ABSOLUTELY full of flowers, overwhelming me with smell. Imagine a small trailer house with a complete greenhouse of floral bouquets filling the kitchen (about 30% of the entire house)! Reluctantly I had to disperse them to family. This smell was quickly overpowered by Dr. Xengs Chinese herbal tea, I tried, really I did, but I just couldn't choke it back. My lack of a glass pot led me to try to use a bowl to boil the tea as prescribed, this led to a broken bowl and a complete infusion of obnoxious Chinese tea smell through the trailer.

Everybody knows that you lose your hair with chemo. Chemotherapy is a cocktail of different drugs that kill fast growing cells. These fast growing cells include your mucous membranes-meaning that the mouth is sore and your sense of smell is extra sensitive. Strong smells of any kind become nauseating. I had a lovely gift of a lavender pillow-only my super nose just couldn't take it.

I really did not enjoy being at home; it was starkly quiet without the kids and a reminder of my domestic ineptitude. I preferred to stay at my parents and have frequent naps with the babies. Paige and I would drift and snuggle throughout the day, definitely a highlight. I was shocked that I could not be up for more than an hour or so without a nap.

Meanwhile, Dusty quit his job. Dusty was working in the movie industry and just started a feature film that would become "The Claim," a dark tale about the gold rush. He quit work to be my memory, my puzzle friend and near constant companion. The Social Workers at the hospital were quick to tell us that most young marriages do not make it through a cancer diagnosis. My fear around this was a knowing that this was going to be a growth time for me and I didn't want to 'out grow' him. My fears were unfounded. We have often said that we feel like were transported 10 years ahead in our marriage, skipping a lot of BS along the way. People say that they will be there in sickness and in health, Dusty proved it. Throughout this ordeal he made me feel special and beautiful, even when I was bald, 110 pounds and had tubes sticking out of me.

Dusty was exceptional at remembering my counts, my drugs and the details of people, allowing me to drift in a drug and positive thinking haze. To put this in perspective he is also a person who hates hospitals, hates to be idle and from the outside appears to be a 'traditional' quiet cowboy.

I fully appreciated the fortitude and generosity of spirit that he showed when I participated in a support group for transplant participants. It was a 6 week support group, and I had read that people who go to support groups survive longer. There were only three of us and I was amazed to listen to their stories of lack of support, one husband had left and the other one had withdrawn emotionally, not even taking a day off of work to pick her up after transplant. Again gratitude was my prevailing emotion.

People often lauded me for my great attitude, but seriously, after only a couple of other people's stories how could I not be? My support force was immense. The entire community seemed to take my diagnosis personally.

Most overwhelming were the prayers, I had notification that there were prayer groups praying for me in all the small towns around me and in every denomination of church as well as at a former workplace and my monthly women's group.

The idea of this much divine intercession influenced my mood and often moved me to tears. There were times that I felt suspended on the well wishes of others and often thought of and sensed angels and divine beings surrounding me.

Don't get me wrong; I was scared, probably in denial and consciously working on managing my thoughts and feelings. My memory though, corroborated by my journal is that this was ever woven with gratitude. My journal during this time is a blend of test after test, who came to visit and what they brought and what side effects I was to expect (you may lose your fingernails). As I sit here now and read it I'm overwhelmed by the complexity of it, I think I was numb during this time, my memory of it is vague. The fear I remember was that depression is very common in transplant patients, I really did not want to be depressed, attached to my sunny disposition and afraid of the darkness.

I was burying my anger and fear at this time, in what I realize now as almost superstitious. Instead of feeling these feelings I was stuffing them and they were coming out as nightmares about losing the kids. Connecting with these feelings and allowing them was a lesson that had not come yet. Despite this, as I said above, gratitude was thread through the tapestry of testing and trials.

I was (am) so grateful to live in Canada, so grateful that I lived in a small town, so grateful to have my little boy and little girl. I was so grateful to have a husband who quit his job to care for me and that we could financially sustain that.

Social workers, Counselors and the spiritual team at the hospital would come in periodically and tears would stream down my face, not in sadness as they often assumed, but at how lucky I was with the things that they wanted to talk about, relationships, childcare and finances. My angst was more existential-why? What's the purpose, what is this meant for, what does it all mean? What am I going to do when I am done?

Although other people lamented on why a healthy, nonsmoking 28 year old would get cancer, I did not. I was just continually in wonderment at how people managed without the supports that I had.

February 17, 2000

A weird thing-I think that this adversity's allowing me to get art, saw a poster of 'The Scream' today and I got it-I still don't know about interpretive dance though.

**My hair started falling out today-just strands, if I get a big chunk I'm going to shave it-that will be SO strange.

This experience definitely 'opened' something in me, a new way of seeing, deeper and expanded.

Chapter 5
Preparing to Be Rescued

The next few months were a blur as they prepared me for the stem cell rescue. The plan was to completely annihilate the cancer-with my immune system as an innocent bystander. Happily the bone marrow that Dr. Li so laboriously checked was free of cancer and I was a perfect candidate to be my own donor.

This was a clinical trial, meaning that it was a research study on people. I saw this as a good thing, they are not going to want their 'guinea pigs' to die. I suspected that their care of me would be painstaking, and it was. I did however feel that I was subjected to every test in the hospital and Dusty became adept at navigating the underground hallways as my personal porter. There was a sense of adventure and 'teammanship' in these ventures that reminds me of 'The Amazing Race'! The Foothills hospital in Calgary is an older hospital, so often these forays were through macabre hallways littered with archaic medical equipment, mastering the maze seemed to give us back a tiny sense of control.

My anger seemed to be reserved for one nurse, the one who had to do the informed consent. I'm sure she was a delightful person; her job was completely to blame. It seemed like daily she would interrupt my reverie of prayer and gratitude to inform me of all the side effects of every drug (pages long). She would arrive with her clipboard, pen and exhaustive lists of horrific side affects and possibilities. It was almost laughable; I don't think there was one of these drugs that didn't CAUSE cancer. I've blocked much it out, I'd impatiently listen to her-ya ya ya-I just want to sign." I left her office each time wanting to scream. Angry that she was making me scared, I now realize that the fear was always there, I had just carefully orchestrated ways to keep it at bay and I resented her reminders that deep down I was terrified.

On February 23 I was admitted to have a central line put in place, I was dreading another procedure with me being awake. The central line would allow them to give me medication and take blood without poking. It consisted of a tube with two entry points hanging from my right upper chest. I hated it. It made me feel like a milk cow and never worked when I needed it. Here was my reaction that day:

> Feb 23, 2000
>
> Admitting day already-although I miss home I am much more focused in here.
>
> Dusty and I were up here at 9:00 and they did the central line. It's hard to describe – it was certainly unpleasant but not as painful as I was anticipating. So far that has been the rule, nothing has been as bad as I expected. Now, tomorrow I'm into the real deal-I think I am ready.
>
> **Affirmation
>
> The chemotherapy is good for me; my doctors and nurses are exceptional people who care for me. I may feel terrible, but it is a state that many encounter and I have the strength to get through it. I will have good days and bad, may I remember the good on the bad and appreciate the good. God and

the power of angels and the hopes, prayer and wishes of my many friends and family are with me.

Jake and Paige are well cared for and are continuing to grow and develop into their wonderful little selves- I am important to them but they will continue to thrive without me for the next two months.

Dusty loves me and needs me and I am a priority I his life.

I love myself and I realize the importance that my life has to the people around me. Healing and curing Lymphoma is my goal at this time. In the midst and for the rest of my life I will serve the common good and treat all people with respect and awe. I will get enough sleep and eat enough and will cherish and protect my earthly body- but my soul is prepared to accept God's will. I believe that God has things for me to learn and do and I pledge to pay attention and to make the most of this degree, this vision quest.**

I'm very tired now. My feelings are mixed. Peace, apprehension, heartsick (for the kids and Dusty), determined, faithful and tired.

My central line is a bit sore, but I don't see that sleeping will be a problem.

God is with me.

**If I'm going to get counseling I should do it in the morning-this is when I am the saddest.

Am I a succulent wild woman? I'm becoming one!

It's scary to face my potential-this is what I want to talk to a counselor about-or clergy-me-

I now have no hair- and I LOVE it!

"You have a great head," "If anyone can do it-you can"- what people are saying about my bald head.

Things I want

Go camping

Be more open with Dusty

Spend more time with Jodi

Take the kids hiking

Show my Mom and Dad how much I love them

SLEEP-all of a sudden I am exhausted.

Kim bought me a pillow-that is SO awesome

The affirmation I wrote that day is one of my favorites. The next day I wrote:

February 24, 2000

My chemo starts in a half hour, I can't wait for it to start so I can stop dreading it.

8:00 Decadron and Zofrin for nausea, allopurinal for possible gouty side effects and to protect my kidneys.

Visualization of Bravery-

Sandra dancing inform of our whole class in our first semester of my Masters' Degree-one of the most moving things I've ever seen- a true woman- made me proud.

My Aunt brought me 6 hats yesterday

Along with the visualization of bravery, an approach I used was to talk with my chemotherapy. I would say, "Thank You, I am choosing to have you, I request that you only go to where you need to and then pass quickly through me." This kept me calm and fortunately I endured only short term and relatively minor side effects. Nausea of course was ever-present, but as I said before, the drugs for managing this have come a long way. The smell of the chemotherapy when it comes out (during urination) is overbearing, but as I smelled it I was always thankful that it was a sign that it was moving through.

I also talked to my body:

Me; how are you?

Body: Thank you so much-I've really tried hard but I'm sorry I let you down-but now I'm getting the help I need.

Me: Don't feel bad Body-I know how hard you have been trying-you are doing great and I love you.

Body: I will do my very best to stay healthy and not have side effects and I will work with the chemo to fight this-it's big, but I'm bigger.

Me: Well, we have body, mind and spirit on side, we should be able to kick this thing.

The plan: 3 chemotherapies, a starter, a conditioner and the big one-followed by the rescue. In the interim I would have a stem cell harvest.

February 26 was the last day of the second chemo. Jake and Paige were in for a visit, a rare treat. On this day I met a cowboy, he had a rodeo jacket on so while he and I stood waiting for a nurse I introduced myself. He was in to see his sister, she had 6 year old twins and was waiting to die. I was so, so sad about this-sad about dying in this institutional place. I found out a week later that she had passed on and resolved not to die there.

As the chemo took effect I had a down day:

> February 28, 2000
>
> My sense of humor has taken a leave of absence-like last time I had a night of nightmares and I'm very weak and down today.
>
> It's one of those "I don't want to do this" days.
>
> I'm losing my desire to see the kids and that really scares me-look at this (very scrawly) I can barely write.
>
> The smell and taste of the chemo is attached to me. I really hate this.

On March 3, God talked to me. I have a strong audible experience. There's no good segue into that. This I recall vividly he said

"Don't think so hard, you don't have to figure things out-they are already figured out,"

And then more quietly

"You just have to be quiet enough to discover."

YOU DON'T HAVE TO FIGURE THINGS OUT, THEY ARE ALREADY FIGURED OUT has stayed with me and offered comfort many times.

Chapter 6
It was the Best of Times...

Back to the treatment, the harvest consisted of GCSF shots, I don't know what that stands for but I responded remarkably, too remarkably. We were required to stay in the city so that I could get these shots daily. Our friends turned their home into a quiet and peaceful healing retreat. I would snuggle on the couch watching TV and Paul would bring me a milkshake every day-obviously pained by my ever skinnier body.

I spent a lot of time in bed, unable to do a lot I continued the meditation visualization that had come to me at the beginning. Laying in stillness on my back, I would call on healers across all time and space naming the ones I could think of and then I would visualize myself lifting into the level of healing-which I visualized about 6 inches above my body. I had not been trained in any of the metaphysical healing that I do now, this was just made up. I would then feel warmth spread from my feet and it would slowly make its way up my body.

One day I was going through this while in my small bedroom at Paul and Beth's when something extraordinary happened. As the warmth was nearing mid body I experienced a jump, a shock, I'm not sure how to describe it but my body jarred and I saw a multicolored geometric pattern in the air above me, my body was flooded with warmth and wellbeing. I kept this to myself. Two years later I went to a psychic with a friend and she said, "the angels healed you, you know" and this incident immediately entered my mind. I really don't know if this was my moment of healing or not, I continued with treatment and over time realized that the why and how were less important than just enjoying my life.

After 4 days of shots of the GCSF in the stomach I was feeling quite short of breathe and just off. We were traveling to the hospital daily and this was one of those 'holy smokes this is a big parking lot' days. I told the nurse right after my daily shot that I felt terrible and luckily she responded. She talked to a doctor over the phone and they decided to send me for an x-ray.

This day showed me that pain happens, but suffering is optional. What on the material, outside of things appeared to be the worst day ever was, emotionally and mentally, one of the best.

Dusty ferried me down to x-ray. The two of us sat for what seemed like an hour in the hallway afterwards. Despite numerous offers for Dusty to just take me, they refused let us leave without a porter. We were sitting in a hallway and at the end of the hallway was a door with a little window. People kept walking by and peeking in at us, one after another. Dusty and I laughed as I provided their dialogue. "Look at that poor girl, hey come look at this, there she is laughing, she has no idea, poor thing."

I didn't have any idea. When a porter finally came and brought us back to the original nurse she said, "oh boy did they want you out of there, your x-ray scared them to death, we are rushing you in for a CT scan." I should have been scared here, but somewhere along the line Dusty and I had picked up a goofy mood, we were like teenagers on a date, and it persisted.

The CT was more definitive-it was not a completely enlarged heart as the x-ray had suggested, but the lining of my heart was full of fluid.

This meant calling the heart surgeon back into work, she was half way home, she and her husband were two of the few heart specialists in Alberta so they lived in Red Deer, 2 hours from Calgary, in between the two major centers where they operated.

Dusty and I went to Unit 57 to await our heart specialist. We were sitting happily doing a puzzle when a sweet young nurse came and asked how we were doing,

"Great" I answered,

"Do you want to go to your room?"

"No, I'm good"

I said, not realizing that it was a request, not a question.

"I am your private nurse, they have called me in just for you"

Wow, I thought- and

"I need you to come to your room to take your vitals."

They had also given me a private room, again with the 'too nice' to be good news. As she was walking me back to my room another nurse came up and stopped her, touching her on the forearm and said in a whispery voice

"how is your patient?" With a 'how bad is it?' tone in here voice.

"I'm right here"

I said, and she almost jumped, apparently I was not aware that I should be looking and acting worse off!

My nurse was great and she, Dusty and I headed into the main tower of the hospital, we were in a completely darkened hallway-everyone gone for the day, it was ominous. We joked that I'd better watch my kidneys. We went to the end of the hall and in a small room there was an ultrasound and some instruments set about. Shortly after arriving a woman physician in street clothes came in. We apologized for making her come back, she was gracious. SO in this tiny room there was the doctor, an assistant, my nurse, Dusty and I. The plan was to stick an instrument (called a pig) into my heart sac and drain it.

Low on assistance, Dusty was enlisted as the doctors helper. We remained jovial despite this being one of the most painful procedures that I endured. They had trouble getting the pig into the heart sac and the scraping of the heart covering hurt a lot. Finally, they succeeded and using a pressurized bottle managed to suck a large quantity of pinky fluid out. Dusty seemed more interested than freaked out and he is still able to recount the procedure in detail.

I carried the large bottle of pinkish fluid back to Unit 57 in my lap, Dusty pushing the wheelchair, and by this time I was very tired, I phoned my parents, who were not very impressed that I hadn't called them in, and finally I collapsed into bed.

The next day my transplant doctor was serious and seemed concerned. He explained that they needed to test the fluid for cancer cells and if it proved to be cancerous they would stop all treatment; that would be it.

Here is the best part; they lost the fluid! It never showed up. I did have to have the heart drained again and had a little bag hooked up for a few days to allow it to continue draining. This second batch proved to be healthy cells. They never did have a reason for this happening, but they stopped the GCSF just in case. I had far fewer shots than the protocol called for but blood work indicated that there were many stem cells floating about and ready to be harvested.

Chapter 7
It was the Worst of Times.

Now to the other extreme, the emotionally worst day.

I woke up fairly optimistic on the day that they were harvesting stem cells, I wasn't too worried about the procedure. This quickly changed when my central line decided not to work. This had been a constant battle, apparently my happy body kept healing over the hole and disabling its ability to allow free flow. The procedure required an open line, they take blood out, put it in a machine that sifts out the stem cells and then put it back into the body.

There was one experienced nurse who could fix it every time and she wasn't working that day. So they tried it a couple of times, nope,

"It won't work, we will just do a femoral line."

WHAT!!! My frustration came out of thinking that they had not tried hard enough and I had had it with procedures. They flushed it a couple of times, but despite my arguing for it they refused to do it the way that the experienced nurse did. That was the moment I lost it. I cried and yelled at the nurses, and this change of character freaked everyone out.

I can clearly remember the mood, the frustration and the belligerence I felt as I was wheeled out of my room and into the basement to put in a femoral line, opening up an artery in my groin to do the stem cell harvest.

I begged the surgeon to put me under for the procedure. I was mentally pissed off and physically exhausted and I would have gotten up and ran away if I could have.

Dusty now tells the story that I was swearing, I don't remember that, but I definitely felt like it. I was really mad that everyone was so nonchalant about the line not working (I cursed it repeatedly, the ugly thing bothered me) and that we will just run a line up your femoral artery-yep, we will just add another hole in your groin, no big deal!

The truth of the procedure is that I was so busy bargaining to be put out that I missed the big event, it was fast and painless. I thanked the doctor profusely and relaxed a little.

I was wheeled on a bed from my room to some place in the basement and up into the main tower. This older part of the hospital had the decor and feeling of the 60 s, think Formica table, metal, something that they use in horror movies now. The harvest room was a cramped space, full of extra equipment and odds and ends and there were 2 or three other people having procedures in the room. My Mom and Dad were there that day and they mirrored my low feelings that day; they were in a state of near panic.

My dad took Dusty aside in the waiting room and expressed his belief that they were probably going to lose me. Maybe this was when the reality of the situation hit the three of us. Dusty was a rock that day, snapping my dad and me out of our negativity and back on track. With me he just listened and portered me around. With my Dad he reminded him that they could never lose me because I would live on in Jake and Paige. Dusty was unwavering with us, but I was happy to hear that he would break down on occasion and talk to our sister in law Lori.

They hooked my new groin line to the machine that removed my blood, stripped it of stem cells and then put it back in, amazing. It was not painful, and they explained that it could take up to 8 hours to get what they needed. After an hour and a half I started to feel edgy, I felt skin crawly and was fantasizing that I would just pull the lines and run away. This thought was persistent so I shared this with a nurse and wow did they go into action; that was the sign that I was losing too much calcium and not doing well with the anti-coagulant. They brought me some milk and the feeling subsided. In the meantime they decided to check the sample they had taken so far, despite having a reduced number of GCSF shots I was kicking out stem cells with vigor. I was done in 90 minutes with stem cells left over in case I ever needed another transplant, a miracle considering the expected 8 hours.

I was unhooked, the line that had finally broke me down was removed and I returned to my room, another step completed.

I can see now in writing this that the difference between the 'best of times' and 'worst of times' days had nothing to do with the actual events, but more to do with my state of mind and expectations. I thought that I 'knew' how the stem cell harvest should go, when it didn't I was sorely disappointed, although no one had any control over how it unfolded. On the day that Dusty and I floated through the 'heart flood' we had no expectations, nothing to compare it with. We were present and in the moment.

There is one little comment in the week before this that I want to reflect on:

I have NOWHERE to cry.

I've already said that this was a great floor with great nurses, so this is in no way reflection on the staff. Throughout my stay I was struck by the lack of a healing atmosphere. There are studies on the healing effect of nature, of color, of music and of relationship. I can see why people turn towards alternative medicine, usually more focused on these things. As I lost weight and felt lonely with my able bodied visitors I wondered at the isolation of us as patients, in the same room but separated by curtains and Canadian politeness. I wondered at what might happen if we were to have family style, communal meals. I wondered at the effect on the nurses at working in the stark atmosphere under fluorescent lights day in and day out. I still wonder. I wondered about the colors and the smells and the lack of music. I know that in alternative healing spaces this sense of healing atmosphere is attended to with extreme care and attention and usually before anything else is considered. Could this really be so hard to integrate? And the food...

In the space between harvesting the cells and my isolation time in the hospital, and after the harvest day freak out I decided to seek some help. My recent Master's Degree put me in touch with some great therapists and modalities. I went for a session of EMDR (eye movement therapy) to try to clear the association that I had with the IV pole.

Every time I'd see an IV pole I would feel instantaneously nauseous, I would avert my eyes, as I was spending much time at the hospital you can see how this would be disconcerting! It was a fascinating session, my eyes followed her hand, back and forth, back and forth and I was invited to shared what came up. I don't remember the details, I know I did some crying and felt better afterwards, and the nausea was much better.

I also sought out personal counseling at the Cancer Center- the psychologist was quiet, smart, caring and experienced and seemed to pick out right away that my angst was existential. What was all of this about? What was I supposed to get out of this? These are the questions I was asking-grateful that my other concerns were taken care of with ease. I came away with a more realistic expectation of my positivity, feeling better about the times when I just wasn't feeling it, letting myself feel it and not judge those negative and down moments. In my own words back then:

> I don't need to be in a state of positive feelings and hope at all times and just because I can handle and cope with all of this shit-I don't have to like it.

This counselor was key to my wellbeing at the time and has subsequently become a cherished friend.

The kids-so, how were the kids up until this point? My parents had them full time, but they (my parents) were also coming to see me every day, so we had a wonderful staff member at the Boys Ranch and friend watching over them. Tammy showered them with love and attention and I'm quite certain they didn't suffer. Their visits to the hospital were infrequent- and generally hard on me, about a month in they stopped kissing me goodbye and were fairly standoffish. Being 1 and 2 they weren't easy to keep occupied in the hospital, they were energetic and wanting to run and touch everything, stressful. Since that first week I had made as much peace with this reality as possible and tried my very best not to fear that they would forget me, it certainly passed through my mind though, and brought deep sadness.

My parents – God Bless Them-also got the kids haircut and bought them what I thought were the dorkiest matching boots, makes me smile to think of those boots. Another incentive to stay alive.

After the apheresis (sucking out of the stem cells) I was able to go home for a bit until my next chemo. I was now on oxygen when in the hospital and I needed another procedure to drain the fluid around my heart-this time they left the drain in and I carried around a little purse like structure to capture the fluid. I realize now I had little awareness of my appearance, it must have been alarming for my family and friends to see me bald, skinny, on oxygen with tubes hanging out of my torso top and bottom. This lack of care of appearance served me well, although at times of health has had me have a sudden awareness in a grocery store without my hair brushed and wearing sweatpants and cowboy boots.

This was the short period before the main event, the high dose chemo for 10 days and then a rescue of stem cells. This would be my longest stay in the hospital and would require isolation (a normal hospital room, only my Mom and Dad and Dusty able to visit).

I remember in this interim period being in the drive thru for McDonalds and calling back to the hospital for my counts. My white blood cells were zero-this means-NO McDonalds and it was back to the house to stay away from people. I was alarmed that I could feel so good with zero white blood cells.

On March 25 I turned 29. I was admitted to the hospital, the celebration was low. I had been having some headaches and after mentioning this the doctor decided that I needed a spinal tap. I had heard often about the pain of a spinal tap, I had avoided having epidurals with my birth because of a fear of a spinal needle and I tried my damnedest to bargain my way out of it. I was terrified.

Unfortunately my arguments, that it was probably from a sore neck, proved to persuade rather than dissuade the need for the testing. I gritted my teeth and again surrendered to what seemed to need to happen. I was too focused on not wanting the procedure to consider that the reason for it was to see if there was cancer in my brain.

It was less painful than I had anticipated and while they were in there they put chemotherapy into the hole, just in case, as even with the dosage of chemotherapy that I was getting it is difficult for it to cross the blood-brain barrier, makes me cringe a bit.

You can imagine my distress when they returned the next day and reported that they had not gotten enough fluid to test. In he went again, a tall robotic resident with no sense of humor or compassion. This time resulted in a spinal headache. I curled up in the middle of bed with the lights off in extreme pain. This was the week of my birthday. For the next 6 years I would find myself low energy and antisocial on my birthdays, it seems to have subsided now, but for a while I seriously considered changing my birthday to the day I received my stem cells.

On my birthday I also received news that my parents best friends (who they had rushed off from in Mexico when I was diagnosed) had lost their son, who was my age, in a bull riding accident. It was a terrible loss and begged the question on whether it is better to go suddenly or with the time to say goodbye. What I've come to find out is that our sense of loss of family is rarely if ever the right time. My parents came to see me on the day of the funeral; Dusty was able to go, but they couldn't stand facing the possibility of burying a child.

Chapter 8
Stem Cells to the Rescue

The nurses made me an amazing calendar for the potential 6 weeks. They took the time to put all the dates and tests and little lady bugs and flowers.

I was admitted to my isolation room, having now covered many of the rooms offered in Unit 57. I tacked up the large pictures of my kids that my Aunt had had done (an amazing gift) and gathered piles of books, handiwork, letters, writing and such to keep me occupied-I wouldn't touch any of them.

My constant companion and true escape became my friend the Nintendo Game Boy and Tetris. Oh Tetris how I love you. In the last year I came across an article showing that Tetris has been proven to prevent Post Traumatic Stress Disorder!! [http://www.1up.com/news/tetris-reduce-post-traumatic-flashbacks-study] I played morning and night. Unable to eat and sleep it was with me at all times.

By this time I had the nurses on notice to not even bring me food-the mere sight of the dusty rose trays would induce vomiting, let alone lifting the lid and having a blast of mixed hospital food steam hit my nasal passage. I ate yogurt, freezies and fruit loops. Yep, some people turn to health food and exercise, I'm here to tell you that Tetris and Fruit Loops were where I was guided.

Coming into this room was strange-knowing that I would not be leaving for possibly weeks. The regime would be 10 consecutive days of chemotherapy followed by my stem cell rescue (the stem cells they had harvested) and then wait to see if they would do their job. My visitors were restricted to Dusty and my parents who all came daily. My perch was in my bed in the middle of the room. My days consisted of giving blood, obsessively taking care of my teeth, sitting in bed playing Tetris and moving to and from the bathroom on occasion.

The bathroom trips, except for the joy of showering were not my favorite time. My bottom hurt sitting on the toilet (no fat-the act of sitting on the toilet left bruises on my skinny behind). And the smell of the chemotherapy moving through is particularly disgusting. I was always thankful to know it was moving through and I continued my visualizations and affirmations that it would go where it was needed and move out quickly.

I was by this time bald, skinny (114 lbs.) on an IV and oxygen with my central lines sticking out of my chest, super attractive. Despite this I had little vanity, I liked the look of my bald head and the constant hydration of the IV had my skin looking youthful, I looked like a cute 12 year old boy.

A few days into the chemo. I developed the mouth sores. The pain of this allowed me to get a drug pump. They started out with Morphine and I was able to get some about every 15 minutes, I didn't realize that they could count the number of times I pushed the button, so they were quite concerned with the pain I was in when I had pushed it 60 times in 10 minutes-it was boredom as I tap, tap, tapped the button with my thumb. The morphine was okay, however 'tipping' became a problem. I both felt that I was tipping out of my bed and I wanted to tip the nurses. I would find myself looking for change when they helped me and another part of my brain would say, "Uh oh, remember when you worked in nursing homes and this would happen-this isn't right." I let them know and they moved me to Decadrone. It was during this time that I remember saying to Dusty "when is it going to get bad-I feel great-I thought this was supposed to be terrible" to which Dusty responded, "honey, you are really high!" So in some ways I think this time, and the whole journey itself was harder on Dusty and my parents than it was with me. I was with myself all the time, I felt it in my bones that I was going to be okay, I knew what was going on AND I was heavily medicated. They were scared, in the dark and sober. My parents had my kids to focus on and Dusty built corrals, big, beautiful corrals every day before coming to visit me and thankfully the angel of a sister in law that he could talk to.

Another special moment of this time was a nurse who needed me, what a gift. I was up at 3 am playing Tetris with one eye open, sipping water through a straw when she came in. I slept sporadically, naps here and there and no actual consistent rest. She sat on my bed and said, "I probably shouldn't do this but I saw in your chart that you are a counselor-can I ask you a question?" and for an hour I had a break from being a cancer patient and got to help her with some boyfriend troubles- it was a welcome reprieve. Getting back into my groove as the helper. Over the years I have seen a consistency of 'self-reliance' in cancer patients, a common personality trait characterized by not needing other people, of being the strong one or the helper. In a way cancer has provided me with a more balanced approach, giving and receiving. In this first journey this small awareness popped up, in the second journey it was monumental.

My kids were not allowed in and I continued to be scared of them forgetting me, they were standoffish when I got out, but it didn't last long. I was too ill to miss them as much as I had anticipated.

I looked forward to more counseling, realizing how very far I was from my feelings and what was motivating me.

The day I received my stem cells back was a landmark, a sign of rebirth. Just as my first chemotherapy had been, it was strangely understated and involved no more than hanging yet another back of something, something on the IV pole!

I survived the days of isolation and when my counts came up to an acceptable level I was moved into a 2 bed room with another woman. She had also had a lymphoma, a stem cell transplant and had two babies. We were strikingly similar in our lives and yet she had very little of the support that I had. She had a loving husband but had to leave her kids with strangers while she was in hospital and he worked. We spoke a little, but she was in for stomach pains. From behind the thin curtain in our small room over the week we were together I listened to her hopes, her deteriorating sense of health and finally the day that the doctors came in and told her that there was a new mass around her kidneys and they were going to do a second stem cell transplant. I came to find out later that she did not make it.

I got grouchy at this time, lashing out at the people closest to me and having little patience with their questions. I even got grouchy at my journal and stopped writing.

The day that I got to leave came quicker than expected with my body bouncing back nicely. I packed up all the things that I had brought to keep myself amused and handed them to Dusty. I was weak by this time. It was a cold, grey and rainy day. I don't know if anything has ever tasted sweeter than that fresh air. I could have stood and felt the breeze on my face for hours, but I was quickly cold and the walk to the truck was a bit of a trek after being in bed for a couple of weeks. It was absolutely a feeling of awe and freedom, one of the gifts of being withheld from normality is the appreciation of it.

We needed to stay nearby and we retreated to our friends' home.

Another strange awareness was going shopping with a friend shortly after exiting the hospital, I had nothing that fit and so we went to the mall. I can completely understand Body

Dysmorphic Disorder, I just couldn't see that I was not a size 9, I tried on 6's to start with, then 4's , a two and finally I bought a size 0 pair of shorts, I didn't even think my bone structure went to that size. Despite knowing this I did not feel different in my body- and I must not have looked at it much because I never did attach to being this small. It is one of the first things that people bring up when they talk about that time though "you were so skinny," I missed it! I overshot 'perfect' a little and am right back to where I started at 150. Having that wee bit extra was beneficial to me then, so I worried about it very little.

After the stem cell transplant I was given time to recover, I spent time at my parents with the kids, napping with them and playing as much as I could. I had been eager to get them back, but the reality was that it was going to be a while before my vitality matched that of a 2 and 3 year old.

I had the kids for a few weeks before radiation started. After a stay at my Mother In Laws Jake got chickenpox, she was unfortunately suffering with shingles, I was alarmed but was told that my titres were good, I couldn't get it. Paige then got followed suit and got them and I started radiation.

All of my joy and bliss in chemotherapy did not transfer through to radiation. I never felt good about it and there were 20 days! I did question the need for it and the radiologist felt that the chances of the cancer returning were high without it, I don't question my decision then, but I would approach it differently now as I believe my intuition may have been correct that it was unnecessary. I ended up with lung damage from the radiation, although after other miraculous healings I am curious whether that is still the case.

5 days a week to the hospital for radiation. Shortly into it I came in and asked to see my nurse, I showed her the marks on my back and sure enough, chickenpox for me too, again I was quickly isolated. Not only this but I had had a small dry circle on my forearm all the way through treatment, it was

assumed to be eczema, it turned out to be ring worm and it went CRAZY, apparently ringworm LOVES radiation. I was a red, hamburger chested mess. I was miserable, I was tired, and dealing with moving home again. It was definitely a transition for Dusty and I, his patience with me being a patient seemed saved for the hospital. One day I was sitting on the coach contemplating the trek to the washroom and he said, "if you would just get your ass off of the couch you would start feeling better," his frustration finally sneaking out. This was a stark contrast to the babying I was getting from my parents. My Dad would have come and carried me to the bathroom if I had called.

The daily trek to the hospital was also taking its toll. My parents insisted on being an hour early, my in laws were either right on time or a bit late, both scenarios stressed me out and the lack of control drove me crazy. One day, having had enough of this I told one that I was going with the other and vice versa and drove myself, a small rebellion and small bit of control on an out of control situation. In hindsight I still hadn't learned about the value of speaking my truth, something I am committed to now, releasing the 'need to please' and 'obligation vibration'.

The outpouring from the community continued, 4 women showed up one day to clean out my entire garden, a big job that I was not allowed to do. This time was a rollercoaster for me, grateful, finding joy in my yard and kids and at the same time feeling tired, owly and traumatized. The ringworm climbed onto my face and my vanity finally kicked in, my face! This too passed.

At this time I think everyone was ready for it to be over and for me the really hard time started. In my journal I had written

"This is the homestretch, but the homestretch is always the hardest part of the race"

I was so right. After months of staying perky and positive my mind started letting the rest filter in. I spent time in bed, in the bathroom and in being alarmed at peoples reactions again. The lines of questioning were "you are fine now right?" nobody seeming to want to hear that I was just now feeling afraid and angry! They were also very intent on me eating and I had no appetite whatsoever. I entered into a support group for transplant patients with Dr. MacRae. There were only three of us, three women and again my blessed life was highlighted. One woman's spouse hadn't taken one day off of work, the other's teens had been remarkably selfish, of course I know this was just fear playing out, but I was grateful for my rings of support. The biggest thing I got out of these 6 weeks was a simple exchange. I was ranting about the fact that when I was honest with my feelings, when I admitted to people that I was scared, mad or depressed that everyone else falls apart and I was sick and tired of being the strong one. The counselor looked me in the eye and said

"So, you want to be honest with your emotions, but you want everyone else to fake it?"

Aha.

Chapter 9
Back to Life, Back To Reality

The next couple of months were topsy-turvy, still many trips to the hospital for tests, walking strange lines between getting back to normal, new normal and absolutely not normal at all. Obsessing over every cough, lump, sniffle, obsessing over a mole that my brother had. It was also a time to reconfigure marriage and parenting with a high level of fatigue, every day I could do a bit more, but I was equally exhausted by the end of each day, definitely not good for our sex life.

In September I went to see a Naturopath, I was committed to health and being healthy. Unfortunately this was a negative experience and I didn't return. She seemed quite angry that I had had chemo (a little late to go back now) and insisted that I needed to go on a severely restricted diet and $1300 worth of supplements and vitamins per month! When I questioned it she said,

"Well, how much do you want to live?"

I felt guilty for my kids and completely overwhelmed, I started to cry and cried all the way home and straight into Dusty's arms. I recounted the entire diet, the supplements, the coffee enema's required and he cut it to the chase.

"Well if that is how your life is going to be why would you even want to live?"

Wham- phew-back to living.   I know that this is not the norm for Naturopaths.

I started therapy with a counselor, an angel therapist, and her love and acceptance for me was exactly what I needed. She quickly got me to realize that I was being unreasonably positive and minimizing what I had been through, I booked Dusty in too!

I also switched acupuncturists at this time. Dr. Xeng had been amazing and I went daily while going through radiation. She took on a student during the time I was there, she was kind, but not gentle! She would lean over the needles and poke them in, drop machines, and I was having needles from head to toe. I started going to a minimalist acupuncturist, using far less needles and less intensity, gentle was the call of this time.

My CT scans were positive and things were looking up, despite a bout in the hospital with pneumonia, I was feeling better and had booked a retreat, I was truly returning to wellness.

August 8, 2000

Cancer

When I first knew you-

You scared me

I had heard about you-

I was aware-

It wasn't all true.

And even though you aren't very nice

I'm not going to love you yet!

I will now let you sit beside me

You've become a part of me

A mentor on life.

You are not going away,
I tried to smile you away,
Push you away, pray and hope you away,
Chemicals and light radiation even,
Part of you may be gone
But a shadow remains-
Beside me, not over me
A screen from which I now see life through-
A new color.
I don't like you, you still scare me,
But I am starting to know you.
You can sit by me,
But I am not sharing my lunch.

September 8, 2000

I now have enough hair for a bad hair day.

A brown rooster tail, right on top!

My appetite was voracious today, I went on birth control pills, I am definitely menopausal.

Life is very good; I am seeing things in an interesting light. This book from Courtney really has me thinking (Return to Love- Marianne Williamson)

October 24, 2000

I've decreased from daily to monthly writing, not because of not having insight and growth but just from letting life carry me away.

From the Therapist – whose sessions continue to renew me and make me thing and my new acupuncturist? I'm really thinking that the balance that I need is just to be more human, more in touch with my feelings and state of being in the moment. I need to let go of worry and over-thinking.

My Sept. 30 CT showed 'marked improvement' in my lungs and my tumor continues to shrink, now down to 5.5 cm.

The day after I found this out I landed up in Oilfields hospital with pneumonia, it knocked the tar out of me. I found it very depressing to go from so much energy to so little again.

In November I took a trip to Kings Fold, a retreat center west of Calgary. Located on a high post overlooking the river and run by a generous and loving Christian group, the Kings Fold is a perfect spot for transformation. The Tapestry Retreat is a 5 day retreat for people dealing with cancer and after a few months at home and dealing with darker thoughts and feelings it was perfect timing for me. There were about 12 of us and it was even more impactful than I had imagined. "Here I am crying and basket weaving in the wilderness" is how I described it! The retreat involved group work, individual counseling and healing activities including yoga, massage and the arts. I ate it all up and enjoyed being away from family and friends and in the company of people who truly understood what I'd been through. Universal themes emerged, doctors rushing in and out, challenges with family and friends and the interplay of hopes, fears and everyday life framed by cancer.

I spent much time alone, quietly holed up with my journal and the voice of poetry in my head.

Here I am
Just here in my life
Not aware
Of who I'm being
Knowing that I
Am not always
Being me
Wondering why
I don't
Let go.
Let go of what?
Yearning to know
The Divine me-
And someday maybe
Introducing her to the rest of the world.

A Minor Procedure

"Relax, don't worry,
Please sign this release-
You could die or be damaged
"It's just a slight chance
A minor procedure"
They say in a trance.
No eye contact,
A hand on the door
Your minute is up

Oh yes you may be
A bit sore.

But no time for questions
Just sign and be good,
A minor procedure
Now relax Yes- you should,
A cut in stomach
A needle in the spine
A tube in your groin
Don't worry- you're fine.
Injections of dye,
Hold your breath and now breathe
A drain in your chest.
Now wait-and no you can't leave
It's not quite enough
We need a bit more-
A minor procedure?
I've heard that before.

What I learned from the women at Tapestry
> We do not have control and trying to
> Over-control is very painful
> Allow people their pain.
> Everyone always needs mothers.
> Being crabby and swearing won't kill you.
> Don't judge a book by its cover- even a bit of cancer hurts.
> Be open to all the signs out there and listen, keep learning.

Speak up and take charge.
Even someone gentle and kind can be insecure.
Love your family.
Cry.

I see the time spent here as another key leap forward in my healing journey, grateful for the time to both share and reflect. I left the weekend emotionally spent. I was stopped for speeding on the way home and I burst into tears, I couldn't and didn't stop until I got home.

My journal from this time concludes that I will be dealing with this forever, I am so glad to say that that is just not true. I still have people ask me "how are you," in a very concerned way and there are times when I am stunned and say, "good, why?" before I remember and say, "OH, that, yes, I'm totally good, Thanks!" [Written before the reoccurrence]

For the first year cancer continued to follow me on a regular basis, regular testing and checkups left me waiting for the other shoe to drop. I was required to go back in time and re do each vaccination as my immune system was brand new! I learned that although going through tough times gives you perspective, it had left me raw and more emotional, taking things harder than I had before. "What doesn't kill you makes you stronger" did not seem true to me. I had a few months of high anxiety and irritability, fueled by adding the 2 and 3 year olds back into my life. The stress led to paranoia, any pain, itchiness or nausea suggesting a return of the cancer. I can't say enough that this was the greatest time of suffering for me- and I'm not sure anybody realized that, silent screams, I wasn't telling anyone. My reserves both emotional and physical were low at this time and cancer was a perseveration in my brain, leading me to continually bring it up in casual conversation as I processed all of it. I found myself compulsively telling strangers what I had gone through.

January 3, 2000

It was a great Christmas. I am learning to live with this ever-present awareness of Cancer. It continues to be an acquaintance that doesn't leave, rather than a friend that I welcome, but (for the moment at least) I am content to ride out the grief cycle and enjoy the anger and sadness for a change. Everyone says it's all about attitude, if they only knew, maybe that's part of my problem?

Details: we had Christmas at home, oh, I'm very proud of myself, my parents went to Mesquite and I had the kids the whole time. I was tired but it was the same fatigue I had before without the kids. Anyway, we had Christmas dinner at TJ and Sheri's and Boxing Day at my Mom and Dads.

And – here we are in Arizona! I'm very thankful for this opportunity (sounds like a speech) I feel alive here; it's a healing and creative place. Probably by the virtue of the vast nothingness of it or maybe I am just exhilarated to be warm.

The way down was very stressful and the cancer and treatment has definitely changed my response to stress. I get very anxious and irritable and I feel out of control.

I was not happy with how we did the trip, but in asking for guidance I am seeing lessons that God's probably been screaming at me forever- plan ahead, speak up, know what you want. It's so stressful for Dusty and I when I fall into the martyr, shrinking violet, and helpless female role. Live and learn, live and learn I am trying to do both.

Anyways, with the stress I had very itchy spot in my lymph nodes, neck, armpits, and groin. I was sure it was back and spread throughout my abdomen. I felt terrible, headachy, tired and overwhelmed. ALL from stress. I'm thinking this because on our final day, when we did what we wanted (which was to go on the kids schedule) I felt unbelievably better. Live and learn, live and learn. It's a great opportunity to rest, enjoy 1 on 1 with the kids and some long overdue one on one with Dusty and I and he and the kids.

An opportunity for me to become my truly creative self. There are even some paintings I would like to do. I'm going to do them as poems first and then ask James what medium would be best for what I am picturing, I have really become interested in art.

Poems of my art

Silent Screams

Silently screaming behind doors of the bathroom stall,
And impossibly heavy, fire resistant doors into the
Hospital washroom.

Silently screaming in the back room with the efficient nurse,
Nodding while the drone of probable and possible side effects
Make you consider that there are things
Worse than dying

Silently screaming when they say-
It's all about your attitude,
How could this happen to you or
Don't worry – you'll be fine.

Silently screaming while the student digs
For a vein and appears
Scared to death
Knowing your diagnosis and trying to put this
Together with the fact that you are the same age.

Silently screaming the 2 million times a
Day when you register and reregister the fact
That you have Cancer

Behind the bathroom stall and
Fire resistant doors, toilet flushing,
Water running--
Why can't anyone hear me?

January 8, 2000

Where and who I am at this point.

I am a mother-

I want to teach and accept, learn and guide, I want to be an example and allow for creativity and self-expression, I want to encourage amazing self-esteem and humility, love for others and all things, knowledge of spirit and oneness and continuity and completeness.

I am a wife-

I want to allow for another's self-expression in my life, have respect and awareness for our two separate paths, encourage self-esteem and personal growth, love unconditionally and set limits and boundaries on what I can accept and be clear about this. Teach when I can and learn when I can.

I am a person on my own path-

I want to be open to guidance from God. I want to be fearless. I want to be decisive, I want to take risks, I want to have love for the world and others, I want to have respect for myself, I want to be gentle, kind and loving to me, I want to speak up.

Energizers

I play with the kids, I laugh with Dusty, I have deep talks with my friends, I read uplifting material or something that touches truth, I am warm and comfortable, drinking hot chocolate, dancing alone in the dark, Spanish Music, Simon and Garfunkel, sitting by the river, I get up the gumption to exercise, writing, learning, pondering, dancing with Dusty, long talks in bed with Dusty, singing Karaoke, entertaining friends at our house, playing cards or board games, shopping by myself, riding horses, spending individual time with my Mom or Dad, being at the cabin, clothing club, reading in bed, eating ham and butter sandwiches, eating chocolate ice cream, getting counseling, having a bath, spending the day with Gayle, classical music, drinking latte with whipped cream, golfing, dusk, Christmas lights, churches, My University friends, Celtic music, the rain, Cinderella stories, nice bedding, my yard, my garden, my tree, books about ancient peoples, candles, 4x4ing, Puerto Vallarta, snow angels (angels in general).

Irritators

White noise, loud music, housecleaning, laundry, the kids in danger, people criticizing me, questioning my judgment, people who are too drunk and trying to play games (literally games like cards or monopoly), my lack of self discipline, too much heavy food, wind, cold showers, being too cold when I am sleeping, being in a situation that I fee is dangerous, slobbering too close kisses, when I gossip, Tom Baker Cancer Center, nurses who can't find a vein, trying to make appts. With my specialist, sad stories on TV, cats sleeping on me, dogs that jump on kids, the perfume department in big stores, knick knacks, too puffy of pillows, no blankets when I'm sleeping, when I resort to spanking.

My one year anniversary came and my reflection continued to be existential with a dose of anger "dammit, I already knew to cherish every moment, that people are what count and not to take things for granted." This thinking moved to knowing over this year and I came to realize that I had NO idea what the purpose might be, it might not have anything to do with me because as time wore on and people became more comfortable they began to share the impact of this time on themselves. It took this full year for the gravity of the situation to sink in.

April 5, 2001

My 1-year anniversary and 30th birthday have come and gone. Interestingly (and sadly) my Birthday was more of a mourning, I felt a real sadness for the 29 year old me laying in the hospital, it was almost the worst time of last year I just didn't feel like celebrating, quite the opposite. I had real turmoil and deep sadness inside rather than the joy that you would expect. The one-year of my stem cell transplant, my new Birthday, and an end to the restrictions on digging in dirt, etc. This was way more exciting, and breakthrough today. I was having supper with a few girls who are having a hard time and I thought, "I am so lucky that I have no big problems" I wouldn't have believed it 6 months ago but Cancer is fading into the background, hallelujah.

My last CT scan went excellent, I lay on the bed and I suddenly had a peaceful, calm feeling and I just knew that everything was okay, and when I went to the doctor I still felt the same way. Dusty took the day off to take me in (which means so much to me) and we got to hear together that the tumor continues to shrink, it was like a weight was lifted.

May 8, 2001

I am getting near the end of my cancer journal and near to the one-year mark from when I finished treatment. I am doing Okay, fear grips me sometimes, when I feel tired or sore or anything that could resemble a sign or a symptom. My resolve to be a better person has strengthened, it is more of a knowing than a consideration. So I work on being in the moment and giving up gossip, and right now I search for depth and simplicity. In my actions, my relationships, my work, my parenting.

Last Wednesday I went to visit my friend Barb (a former nun that I met at Tapestry retreat). It was great to see her and she asked me "what gifts has Cancer given to you?" Well, I hadn't really taken the time to think of it, being a little crabby about the whole Cancer thing still.

So here goes...

Because I had Cancer, I know who my true friends are, I understand art, I have met some amazing people, I've been cared for thoroughly, my relationship with Dusty is deeper, my attachment to the kids is healthier, I have a sense of myself outside of those two roles, I have read life changing books that I never would have read otherwise, I'm a better housekeeper and understand the comfort of orderliness, good food and a soothing atmosphere, the kids have an amazing relationship with my Mom and Dad, I am closer to my other family members, I understand pain and suffering to a greater degree and have felt, struggled with and learned from anger and sadness, learning to look after myself, self-awareness health wise (still learning how to pace myself), closer relationship with God, clarity, poetry, Tapestry and the confidence it gave me in my own creativity and finally the grace and helpfulness of my wonderful friends.

So, this is life on the other side, like a mountain I was much better at seeing the big picture from the top. I'm full time mommy, working 2 days per week and very busy, it's great but I find it a bit unsettling to be away from that high of hope and joy that sustained me through my treatment. I still have it but I am once again involved in the mundane world of petty jealousies, gossip, nastiness and negativism that I have lost the stomach for. I can no longer be guilted into doing things I don't want to but gossip can send me praying for forgiveness in a heartbeat. Trying to listen more and speak less, really enjoying my relationships, I am ready to put effort into my marriage, I want laughter and caring and passion.

Dusty has been so amazing at loving me through this and constantly affirming my womanliness, although at times a lot of pressure, all and all I'm sure this has been quite a boon to my self-esteem (whatever a boon is).

I love my life and I want it and for the time being God is allowing that. God's will be done; well I know it and aspire to live like it. It is difficult to embrace if it means leaving here any time soon. I have the direct messages from his angels saying that I will be living it for a while yet- and I believe it.

On to greener pastures...

The year after treatment was spent recovering, my head was full of poetry in this time and the poems say more than my paragraphs ever could.

June 14, 2001

How to Live

Make each day long-
With grand gestures and
Humongous dreams,
With large movements and
Delicate moments.
Live by laughing hard,
Smiling in wonder.
Want everything,
Be kind and generous and
Want everything for everybody else too.
Cling to hope,
Be irrational-
Notice things,
Create,
EN-JOY,
Hug people and look into their eyes,
Reach out and Reach in.
Listen to yourself-
Move to music,

Try to persuade people with happy thoughts.
GET MAD,
Get sad,
And let it go.
Forgive-especially yourself.
No regret,
No worry,
Live   NOW.
Unconditional Positive Regard.
Believe people,
Surround yourself with babies,
Play,
Trust,
Connect, be quiet, be still-
Talk to God,
Listen to God.
Ask for help,
Enjoy helping.
Listen to old people,
Golf,
A lot.
Play games and want to win,
Marvel at our world,
Entertain,
Be thankful,
Collect interesting friends,
Love your family,

Please yourself,
Breathe Deeply,
Practice Caring,
Engage in Humanity,
Vibrate at the frequency of rain.

July 10, 2001

The Edge

Standing on the edge-
Everything so clear.
What makes sense?
What is important?
Life stands before me stripped of illusion.

And as I slip back-
Away from imminent death,
Or rather back to my illusion of safety
The perception of endless life.
Lines become hazy and
Petty annoyance and confusion reenter
Negativity finds me on this false floor.

My heart years for the honesty,
The TRUTH of living in the moment.

Gone are open, deep conversations
With loved ones,
In their place-shallow gossip, complaining that knows no end.

In irony I grieve the loss of illness and
Learn to live again with the 'living'.

Chapter 10
11 Years and Counting

What I thought was the ending...

So here I am 11 years later, mostly amazed at the consistency of my desires, depth and simplicity, which I have examined in ever increasing complexity and dimension. A couple of years after treatment I was at the Cancer Center for a checkup when I noticed my file, super large file, was sitting open. The page it was open to had the words "Prognosis: Poor" at the top and I had signed it. Thank goodness, I don't remember signing it.

At the 5 year mark I was no longer required to submit myself to yearly testing. I celebrated that year with a head shave and barn dance event to raise money for the Tapestry Retreat. I had grown my hair for the year and several friends joined me in pledging theirs. Once again I was overwhelmed by the support of my family, friends and community and it was a fun success.

Shortly after that however I began to feel ill, tired and I began to worry. I was sitting at some girlfriends and they were talking about how they knew that they were pregnant and BAM- What? That was exactly how I felt! I had now been in menopause for 5 years, I had had some minor spotting a couple of times, but when I questioned my Ob/Gyn she patted my hand and said "Sorry Dear, you will never be able to get pregnant again."

I left my girlfriends and searched the city frantically for a pharmacy. There was none to be found so the next day I found myself standing in front of a row of tests, finally just picking one randomly. I took the test and sure enough, two lines, I was shocked and happy. I waited until Dusty got home to share the news, I wanted to see his face, he didn't even know that I was suspicious. I showed him the stick and he said "no, we can't be," "we CAN'T," and then "Who's going to ski with Paige?"

Jake and Paige were now 8 and 9 and quite independent. I was completely excited, but it took a while for Dusty to jump on the 'Happy Miracle' bus. It was incredibly fun to tell everyone, everyone except for my Mom, I knew that she would NOT be excited. Not because she wasn't supportive, but the cancer journey had been just about enough worrying for her in this lifetime.

The day that I told my doctor (the same one who first suspected cancer) was a highlight. She explained to me that she was a bit irritated that the front desk had made a mistake and put "Fawna Bews-Prenatal", then she went to my file and saw that I'd already been in and seen another doctor a couple of times. She was in complete amazement, when I said "What are the odds" she said, "there are no odds; this is a miracle."

The pregnancy progressed and I tried to keep worries about the effects of chemo on my eggs and body and the effects of radiation on my breasts at bay. It wasn't until after the birth that my doctor shared that he too had had his reservations.

On March 6, 2006, 6 days overdue, I was induced. Labor progressed slowly. As with my other kids I had the company of my husband and Mom, adding my sister in law Shannon this time. I had had the honor of attending Shannon's last birth and was happy to return the favor!

The baby was 'sunny side up' and after hours of laboring the delivering doctor decided that I should be sent to the city.

The actual contractions were difficult, managed without meditations and with pressure on my sacrum and hips, a two person job shared by my three helpers! This arrangement was instinctual and made the pain manageable. In between contractions I was fairly blissed out, similar to how I had come through cancer treatment. We laughed and enjoyed one another and enjoyed the amount of times that Johnny Cash's "Burning Ring of Fire" came on the radio by the bed.

So I calmly headed out in an ambulance, subcontracting the stress and worry to my mom. They wanted to do a C-section but the doctor gave me one hour to do what I needed to do to get this baby out, he said, "right now it is your decision, in one hour I will make the decision."

My other two children had been born with me upright and I just felt best like this. I tried to labor laying in the bed as asked, but after too much discomfort and no progress I begged to stand up. The nurse looked much stressed but let me stand and use my team as we had been doing all day, two more big contractions and all hell broke loose, he moved and I went nuts.

After some mayhem Gus Thomas Ross Bews, our miracle, came into the world. Healthy and robust with no need for the massive neonatal team that descended on the room.

I was back home again in 10 hours and we haven't looked back. I enjoyed informing my Ob/Gyn and sent the Bone Marrow Transplant a picture and a note questioning their infertility claims.

Looking back on the last 11 years I see that I have been studying and searching to find the peace of those hospital months. I have read thousands of self-help and spirituality books, taken workshop after workshop and have finally found myself back in that place. Pain happens and suffering is optional, always for me a product of, as author Byron Katie puts it "arguing with what is".

Centered, happy and grateful I look forward to the next chapters.

And then it happened...

"Fuck, fuck, fuck, fuck, fuck," this was Dusty and I's reaction to the Ear, Nose, and Throat specialist. He, in a first and 5 minute conversation had the dubious honor of delivering the message, the cancer is back. The call from the cancer centre was a clue, but I think we were still holding to the small hope that it was a polyp, a benign polyp.

Journey Two

Chapter 11
Here we go again

In 2011 I was plagued by sore throats, one after another, doctor visit after doctor visit, alternative health care provider after alternative health care provider. Using every tool in my arsenal I fought to have control over this body. At the same time laughing at the amount of tools I'd accumulated; affirmations, energy work, spiritual techniques, surrendered and then picked up my weapons again and again. My mind had shifted dramatically at this point, believing that all causes are in the mind and yet having a hell of a time applying this belief.

I saw my Doctor in September, October and in November and had on again off again diagnosis of strep throat. At November's appointment I expressed my concern "this is eerily similar" I said, not believing it myself, but saying it nonetheless, "I'm losing weight and this has really been going on for a long time." She sent me for a chest xray and I was happy to assure my parents that it was negative. Bloodwork negative as well.

After trying a strong antibiotic for 'strep' I ended up in the emergency room, I couldn't't keep it down. The emergency room doctor let me know that the strep test was negative anyway so I could quit. I told him that my throat had been hurting for months now and he said, "It can't hurt that bad if you've been putting up with it for months." This is when I quit going to the doctor. My conspiracy of denial was reinforced.

In January I decided to give acupuncture and Chinese medicine a really thorough effort (I didn't't even think about the fact that this is what I did in 1999 as well). The acupuncturist was great but her face was grave after taking pulses, looking at my tongue. She was concerned about how very sick I seemed, how little health I had from a Chinese Medicine perspective. I didn't't want to hear this. I implored her to be positive and when after 3 sessions I wasn't improving she suggested I see the doctor again. The look on her face triggered something in me. I cried, I spoke tersely to her, I was mad. I was mad that she was not being hopeful, I saw the look on her face that I saw on my best friend Suzi and my Mom and I didn't like it one bit. I stopped going. I was continuing to project my fears outside of myself and despite knowing better I did not listen to the invitation to become still and go inside.

I booked into the doctor, this time there was a discernable mass in right nostril. I obsessively checked it several times a day, grey, a little shiny. If front of the mirror I would shine the flashlight up my nose and implore Dusty to "look, look at that, I see something." I had self-diagnosed it, from the internet, as a polyp. When my doctor looked at it she said, "Oh My God- that is Gross! Why didn't you come in sooner?" I said, "I did." She told me she would book me in for an ENT.

In the next three weeks, it went wild. The mass grew and changed the shape of my nose, it began to grow right out of the right nostril. When a bump popped out on my neck the jig was up, I called my doctor's office and said I either had to see the ENT or I was going to Emergency.

I was miserable. Completely stuffed up, not sleeping, discharge coming from my right tear duct. I was also working very hard. Our family business had acquired the lease of an Inn in August of 2011, seemed like the perfect option for our oldest boys. Since 1975 we had been running a group home for kids, in that time we had often come up against a difficulty finding homes for the older boys once they were too old for us. The opportunity to lease a 7 bedroom space across the road seemed too good to be true, it was. We leapt before we looked and our licensing body didn't agree with our great idea. This left us in the position of running an Inn. To be honest it was a crazy time, full of work and me not feeling well but full of fun and joy at the same time. The woman who came to help me run the Inn, well, she had come to work with the boys but luckily she was flexible too, she and I quickly felt like sisters. The people who came through the Inn were interesting, inspiring and despite one disaster after another we both felt that it was 'meant to be." This was a time and energy consuming position on top of my other job and the life of wife and mother to three. I was exhausted. I was also arrogant about the state of my intuition and 'connectedness' and really didn't see the seriousness of the situation. At the same time, the forgiveness exercises and inner work that I was able to do was intense and I was able to see layers and layers of 'beliefs' that were not helpful to me. As in the first journey there were two stories happening; the inner and the outer.

The doctor's office called that they had an appointment with the ENT in the next week. My mom came with me to the doctor, still in denial, still nonchalant, still using every spiritual concept available to try to heal myself and to stay peaceful throughout. I was fairly cheerful. The appointment was long and I spent it texting my most psychic friend, we were both convinced it was benign. She kept me company while the freezing took effect, laughing at me sending her pictures of the gauze up my nose. The biopsy was made easy by the protrusion of the mass. The young doctor was fantastic, perfect mix of confidence and concern. Although I expected that they would do a biopsy, when I texted it to my

Mom in the waiting room I could sense her concern right through the text. Her concern was eclipsed by my Dad's panic, he burst into tears at the mention of the word 'biopsy' after calling to see why we were taking so long.

Before we got the results we had a call for an appointment at Tom Baker Centre, the Cancer Centre. Dusty came with me for the results of the biopsy, in the short period (5 days) that it took for the results to come back another mass had come through the roof of my mouth. Eating became even more difficult. Our doctor's appointment was less than 5 minutes long. I can't even imagine what it's like to have to meet someone and have only one thing to say, "Yes, it's a recurrence of your cancer and here are the dates for your CT scan and cancer Centre appointment." We left the office swearing, both of us, fuck, fuck, and fuck. I burst out crying before we got to the car. I felt so bad, so, so sorry. I felt so bad for my Mom and Dad and so bad for our kids and so bad for Dusty. I felt so very guilty. At the same time that I was feeling this I was also watching it and aware of how very crazy that this was my initial feeling, guilt and a heavy feeling that has always plagued me, the feeling that I was the emotional caretaker of my entire family (everyone in fact), an impossible and irrational assignment.

Dusty's reaction was more focused on having to watch me go through treatment again.

We had already made plans to have lunch with friends, so in a foul black mood, lightened only slightly with morose humor we met our friends, who later shared that they were a bit traumatized by the event! By the time we got home we had both reconciled to the fact that we were jumping in again, I told the older kids right away and they were fairly nonchalant. "That Sucks Mom," "You will beat it again." I agreed with them. I didn't tell our 6 year old, we explained things as we went along but I didn't have a sense that it would be helpful to go into a long explanation with him.

Where my journal was a constant companion during cancer event A, the internet and Facebook were there for me for cancer event B. Instead of private journaling I blogged. Here is the first one. The coming out.

Chapter 12
A New World
FACEBOOK and BLOGGER

Watching Cancer through Fawna's Groovy Miracle Goggles
4/1/12

3 days???? This could be a book of a blog over just the past three days.
I guess going with what is happening now, the recent news that we are experiencing a recurrence of Non-Hodgkin's Lymphoma changes the face of this blog somewhat. I may have to change the name to EveryMinute Aha-it has been a wild ride already.
A bit of background, in 2000 when I was 28 and Jake and Paige were 1 and 2 we were shocked to find ourselves spending months attending to and healing from a Stage IV Non-Hodgkin's Lymphoma. Treatment consisted of High Dose Chemo with a Stem Cell Rescue, Radiation, and Chinese Medicine with Acupuncture, Prayer, prayer, prayer, meditation, self-inquiry and other mind taming tricks. I am using plurals here as it was definitely not a solo journey. My family, friends and community seemed to take the whole thing as a personal affront. The support was beyond words.
Fast forward 12 years and we are back in the saddle again (did I like this horse or what)? In the meantime we have enjoyed great health, to the point of having a Miracle baby and forgetting at times why people would ask 'how is your health?'
I have been dealing with a sore throat for almost a year, intensifying in September when I began to go to the doctor to see what the heck was going on. After several visits yielded

no action or information I tried Acupuncture, Energy Healing, and just about every trick in my bag of magic.

I have to mention here that my point of view may be different to some. In October I finished the workbook for A Course In Miracles and this, combined with 12 + years of seeking, led to the direct experience of Spirit within. This had been a regular occurrence during the first trek with Cancer, as a gift of Grace rather than a state that I could enter regularly. Due to this the past few months, while on the outside looking like I have been 'suffering' or ill, have been tremendously powerful in my journey to know my True Self.

To be brief in this initial blog as it is more about just getting the information out there, I noticed layers and layers of control, of self-hate, of judgement and of beliefs in separation. My goal is peace of mind, so while in physical appearance moving backwards I have been experiencing bounds of healing in the mind.

Details: after months of trying everything to feel better I returned to my general practitioner at the beginning of March. In February I had developed a mass in my nose that I was calling a polyp (I googled it), the doctor seemed horrified and quickly referred me to an ENT. I waited a week and a half to hear back and bam, the polyp seemed to take a growth spurt, adding on another growth in my neck. At this point I called and said I thought maybe we were getting to emergency stage. They reacted.

On the 21 of March I saw an ear, nose and throat doctor, he did a biopsy and ordered a CT scan. By the following Tuesday the results were in.

And now we are into the past three days. Thursday, Dusty and I returned to the ENT who had the unenviable position of telling me that it was an aggressive recurrence of the Lymphoma and that he had already arranged for us to be at the Cancer Centre the next day.

I was crying before we left the office, but observing at the same time, no judgement in the observing but noticing that my sadness was an overwhelming guilt "how could I have done this again," sadness that I had to give this news to my parents and my kids...

We blew out quite a few F-bombs as the information sunk in. We began to put the word out and it has been a wildfire ever since. As I processed the guilt, the fear thoughts, the threats on the inside, we joined friends for lunch and went through the motions on the outside. Told our families, cried a bit more, and talked to one another.

I put the word out to my healer friends and a few were immediately called to action. Notably, Velva Dawn Silver Hughes, Stacy Sully, Nouk Sanchez and Gayle Fathoullin. Within a couple of hours I had energy treatments, healing circles and cutting edge mind healing information coming my way, childcare for the next day fell into place easily (thank you Tracy, Mom and Dad). I realize that there have also been anonymous light workers who went into action immediately.

I told Jake and Paige that night, they were amazing, Gus is 6 so we will let him know as we go along.

Sinking into bed that night we were pretty much shocked (probably still there now).

Friday morning was a GORGEOUS sunset and we trekked into the city, ready for whatever. The Doctors were amazing and looked like children on Christmas morning when we told them that we thought I had extra stem cells stored there. As it had been rapid they did a Bone Marrow Biopsy, which I did not suffer with, and made the current plan which is full CT scan on Tuesday and Chemotherapy starting on April 9. In the meantime they will meet with their team and decide what to do in this "extremely unusual" case.

In the midst of this I continue my mind watching (often in the middle of the night) I believe in spontaneous healing and miracles so I continued to be bit perplexed that I had done so much inside work (where I believe the problem starts) and nothing was changing. I had gotten the message several times to "pull it out by the root" but apparently hadn't gotten to the root yet. What I noticed Friday morning was a belief that the 'doctors' would save me. Nothing wrong with this, but standing in the way of a Miracle. The quality of this belief was fear rather than faith, a belief in my victimhood, good to see and ask to see it correctly.

Dusty and I were 'punchy' at the doctor, in the car and in the pub where we met my brother (who had texted that he had heard that beer cures Cancer, my brother is not a doctor- please do not use this as medical advice). Dark humour punctuated the day.

I had a powerful long distance energy treatment with Stacy Sully that evening (message me if you want more details) and spent the evening with friends.

Saturday was crazy as the healing and helping forces around me went onto high alert. Notably a healing circle to coincide with Earth hour was organized (I felt it, thank you), I met with some Mighty Companions, spiritual teacher and student friends online, and at noon I got a phone call. The idea of changing my diet had been sprinkling in and I was paying attention, at the same time I was getting the message to give no effort, do what was easily given.

Taking a step out of the blog. In the years between cancer events I had spent hours poring over spiritual and self-help texts. My big question was 'how come on the worst of days I still felt good and at good times I would feel bad'. I was struck by the fact that the external circumstances did not always match the experience. After having tremendous success in regaining vitality after Cranial-Sacral treatment, and having had angelic experiences during this time I also deeply explored and trained in energy healing and exoteric practices. I had come to a place of wide ranging knowledge and the early hints of direct awareness, direct contact with the divine, most often showing up as the Holy Spirit or Jesus, with a support cast of other Divine characters. When I write in my blog about 'getting the message' this was coming in as a 'knowing' or a sense, I would "what am I to do" and would get a fairly clear idea pop into my awareness. In between the time of the CT scan and the trip to the Cancer center another part of the tumor burst through the roof of my mouth. I had no idea when the tumor had invaded the entirety of my sinuses, coming perilously close to the eye socket and brain stem. Back to the blog.

Part of what has come up over the past few months is how I've built a life around me to be 'needed'. Everyone needed me (ha ha). Letting go of that has been a healing and a relief- and it continues. So on Saturday morning I was committed to allowing, receiving and 'saying YES'.

At noonish on Saturday Velva Dawn called me with an urgency. She had recently come across the work of Medical Intuitive and Hay House Author Caroline M. Sutherland. Velva Dawn felt guided to buy me a reading with her, but it wouldn't't go through. Not being able to get it to work she emailed Caroline, expecting to hear from a secretary or representative in a few days. She went back to her taxes and almost immediately had a return email. It was Caroline Sutherland, instructing her to call right away. Dawn called her and Caroline was straight to the point "Drive over there and get her to call, I will do a reading now." Velva Dawn called me, gave the short version and was here 10 minutes later. We called right away and without a pause Caroline began downloading a diet and treatment regime, it took all of Velva Dawn's typing skills to keep up. It was fast, effortless, and more important felt entirely divinely guided.

I have resisted diet changes in the past. During the first Cancer bout I was not guided, prompted or moved to make any changes and enjoyed Fruit Loops cereal for most of my healing time. I say this to emphasize that my belief is that no answer is the answer, go as you are guided.

No Milk, No sugar, No Wheat, No Caffeine were the first 4 things. Velva Dawn took it all down and went to town for supplies, only one item could not be found and she immediately thought of another friend who picked it up and drove it directly to my house, 2 hours away! No effort on my part (other than to fully receive, yikes).

My next two dear guests, Jodi and Shannon, both family and friends brought all the mix-in's for paralyzers, goodies, and Tiramisu. Normally I would have dove into this with gusto- but there was no urge what so ever! Confirmation. I felt a slight pull to people please and not tell them that I wasn't eating sugar, an old pattern that I was particularly good at. I resisted and let them know and they happily consumed some, leaving the rest for my family to enjoy.

I put the news out on Facebook and continue to be amazed with the words, the sentiments, the support, the witness's to the fact that we are all connected.

Miracles continue, I had awareness of the Healing Circle, dinner arrived, and groceries arrived.

My final thoughts, or this is going to be excessively long, is just to see the 'payoff' of being sick. I noticed this last time, but this time I am committed to enjoying the openness, the permission to follow my heart, the permission to rest, the permission to speak your mind that comes with a life threatening illness, I want to enjoy all of this beyond the sickness and thereby give it no reason to return. If you want to know where my mind is going please watch this interview with Nouk Sanchez www.undoing-the-ego.org, we do not need to suffer, we do not need to get sick and we do not need to die (!).

I love you, and I am so happy to share the Miracles. I have found that often people are imagining me suffering while I am basking in the amazingness. No need to suffer. How am I now? I have a visible bulge on the right nostril and a visible large mass filling that nostril, there is a noticeable lump on the left side of my neck, the roof of my mouth and the back of my throat. I have no pain and I am at Peace (other than the 6 year old who wants the computer NOW).

The response on Facebook and to the blog were overwhelming. It was such an easy way to keep everyone in the loop and it reinforced this feeling I'd been having that this cancer was not 'personal' and that we were very much in it all together. I stopped working immediately and my Mom let the lease go on the Inn.

Chapter 13
CT and little tears
4/3/12

The outpouring of support on Facebook, the phone calls, texts and for the blog have been uplifting. Overwhelming would suggest that it is difficult and the only difficulty I've had is the feeling that everybody should get the chance to have this much love showered on them, but without the cancer part.

I am sitting here in my bed with the dog rolled up in a ball beside me, my mouth still has the taste of the 'selenium', the contrast liquid for the CT scan.

The day started early, we were lucky enough to be booked into High River Hospital so my Mom and Dad accompanied me. I haven't seen them since Friday and these past 5 days seem like a month! I was able to catch up with my Mom while I spent 2 hours drinking 4 litres of a tasteless liquid, I think the aftertaste is from the injected version.

When I was well and full bloated it was time to go in, I took advantage of the unlimited hot blankets, mmmmmm. Just before I went in I was wrapped up in a brand new hot towel and after a cheerful morning of chatting I had a sudden picture of snuggling with the kids in bed. Well, then came the waterworks. Instead of trying to choke them back I just sat in observer status, let them fall while I changed into a gown, cut the feather out of my hair, put on an attractive hair cover and while I laid and had the IV started. The technician went about her business, with me but not saying anything, and I believe she may have wiped a tear too. While I was laying on the table, head in the machine, I looked at the fact that the tears were like watching a movie so programmed for those emotional musical flashbacks. I realized that the sadness was about being 'gone', losing the good times, losing the people. No judgement, but truthfully one of several possibilities and not inevitable by any means.

Just watching and not stuffing (my normal approach) proved to be useful, as I sit here now and think of the same scene I do not have the same reaction at all, I feel calm and peaceful. I also realized that this moment in the warm blanket was perhaps one of the few moments I have been alone since Thursday. Twelve years ago when I went through this I would ONLY cry when I was alone: Here is a poem from that time:

Silent Screams

Silently screaming behind doors of the bathroom stall,
And impossibly heavy, fire resistant doors into the
Hospital washroom.

Silently screaming in the back room with the efficient nurse,
Nodding while the drone of probable and possible side effects
Make you consider that there are things
Worse than dying

Silently screaming when they say-
It's all about your attitude,
How could this happen to you or
Don't worry – you'll be fine.

Silently screaming while the student digs
For a vein and appears
Scared to death
Knowing your diagnosis and trying to put this
Together with the fact that you are the same age.

Silently screaming the 2 million times a
Day when you register and re-register the fact
That you have Cancer

Behind the bathroom stall and
Fire resistant doors, toilet flushing,
Water running--
Why can't anyone hear me?

So, this time, I am not taking that same approach, the good suffering no longer serves me.

The rest of the test went without incident, hold your breath, now breathe, repeat. The IV contrast makes you warm and fuzzy, a strange feeling but not a terrible side effect.
The rest of the day was uneventful and now we sit and wait to hear about results, we already know that it has been named as a B-cell Lymphoma but waiting to hear what stage. It doesn't really make any difference to me at this point.
I am definitely feeling the positive effects of all the energy work, healing circles and prayers. Glad to have such a big posse in this.

Chapter 14
Reactions
4/5/12

As I wade into the Western Medical System every treatment is accompanied by a list of "possible side effects," often they will make me laugh out loud-wondering- really? This is good for me?
What I've been thinking about though are other types of reactions, other side effects. Twelve years ago I remember the shock of 'other peoples' reactions. Prepared this time I've been able to have compassion and patience that I didn't't always feel before.
The word cancer, the thought of a mother dying, and whatever other stories come up for people inherently seem to lead to fear. This fear expresses itself in a few different ways, the fighters and the flighters. Mad at the doctors for not catching it sooner, quick to need to 'do' something or suggest something, the fighters want to get right in there. The flighters either shut down, avoid, deflect and feel terrible in the process. Unfortunately, I'm having piles of friends judging themselves as selfish.
The thing is, to me selfish is most helpful. How you react is a goldmine for 'waking up'. For stopping being in a rut of continuing the same pattern over and over. My Truth is that (and this may be hard to wrap the head around) but that you are not sad/mad/frustrated about me, or this story, these emotions are there just waiting to be expressed. They are attached to a tale, the tale is attached to belief and usually that belief has "unintended side effects."

I'm inviting everyone to be selfish, take a look at the 'what is going on here'. Become quiet and follow the emotion back. Looking at the behind the scenes drama going on allows us to bring it to the light, the light takes the power and you can lean into being 'responsive' vs. 'reactive'.
What does this look like in practice? Here's what has been helpful to me.
When I got my diagnosis my first reaction was tears, I was sad, I felt SO, SO bad. As I looked at it, watched what was going on, I saw the following:
"How could I have done this?"
"How could I do this to my parents, my kids, my friends?"
"It's all my fault"
"If only I had pushed harder"
So sadness was guilt, guilt had this story of how I have done something wrong. Then I look for the belief, the belief that I saw here was "I am responsible to keep everyone happy", I've seen this one in me before. I sat with it. I applied the work of Byron Katie http://www.thework.com
Now I make sure that I am gentle and kind with myself, this is not an indictment, but an investigation.
This belief that I am responsible to keep everyone happy has the following side effects:
1. Manipulative behaviour
2. Fake happiness
3. Emotion stuffing
4. Rescuing
5. Greasy discharge (just kidding, that one just always makes me laugh)
Okay, now what. After a thorough look it usually has lost much it's power, I ask the Holy Spirit to look at it with me, forgive myself, and wait, if I'm still I will usually get an answer of a feeling of peace, of calm or words "you are innocent" "happiness comes from the inside"
I will also realize that all fear is in the past or future, I think I might feel less afraid now that the diagnosis has been made, I'm not afraid that I might have cancer and have to tell

everyone. I have it, everyone's been great, and I am not entertaining dying at this point.

I'm totally cool with the crying, the anger, the pain that is showing up, all good, I just invite you to join me in 'erasing' some of these beliefs and set yourself free.

Freedom from suffering- mmmm-that sounds good to me.

Would love to hear your thoughts on this one, it's trippy to change the idea that, "I am sad because...something outside" to "I am not sad for the reason I think, where is this coming from Truly?".

Let's do this together. Minga!!!!

Minga-

"The concept of Minga has existed since before Incan rule. Minga is the gathering of community members to complete a task that benefits all of the community. It is considered each individuals' obligation to the community."

(www.alishungufoundation.com/Minga/index.html)

Thank You to my Cousin Jodi for introducing me to the idea of Minga after hearing Craig Kielburger (founder of Free the Children).

As this blog indicates, again, a certain strangeness arose out of the reactions of others. My premise by this time was that others are a reflection of ourselves and what I was seeing in friends and family was indicative of the ranges of feelings that seem to come up from cancer but are always there waiting to be expressed. Cancer acts as a swift reality check, an opportunity to deeply feel the fear and guilt that is otherwise masked in the business of life, the busyness that we have created.

Chapter 15
Laying It All Out There
4/12/12

I realize as I sit here that I feel a bit of pressure to write something good! haha-there- I'll just shake that off and continue to ask Holy Spirit to just join me here and share what seems helpful to share.
I'm sitting in my bed, been here for the past three days, amazing how you can stay in the same space and still experience the range of emotions that often seems to go with moving about in the world.
I had Chemotherapy on Monday, I'm happy that my friend Janet Pliszka[who invited me to play at recess in Grade 5 on my first day at Longview School making me feel warm and welcome, as opposed to my brothers week of 'who is the toughest in Grade 4'Thanks Janet], I'm happy that Janet could come, we were both just 'feeling it'. I did regret not having more pictures of the process last time. I'm looking forward to Janet's blog.
For Dusty and I the day was uneventful, I was hooked up to the IV from 9:30 to about 4:00-with no adverse reactions. Had a nap, played Tetris, looked at Facebook, eavesdropped on the nurses conversations, not much of anything really. I felt calm and peaceful, wondered what everyone else's story was, which is how I usually feel in a group of strangers. Dusty was patient, got me food and sat in the corner on a hard chair. Luckily he listened to my medication instructions as they seemed to have escaped me.
I felt fine until Monday night and the nausea hit, gross taste in my mouth, general yuckiness (autocorrected to luckiness,

nice)! I had a meeting on Tuesday at the Ranch So I got dressed, looked good and went from there to a beautiful Reiki treatment with Reiki Master and loving Earth Mother Sandy Day. The treatment with Sandy was great, she sent love to the cancer saying, "I know that it is probably hard for you to do right now" and then exclaimed on all the light and love and 'high vibration' despite everything. I think we are all feeling that (and I can't help think that you are all contributing, thank you).

My Dad drove me to and from the appointment, I'm learning to ask for what I need. Another sidebar, today I wanted Hamburger soup and asked for it, my brother in law made it for me, don't know why but that totally warms my heart.

Okay, details aside, here is what I want to share and I really want to do it Justice. I capitalized that on purpose, when I capitalize it's usually because it has to do with Truth to me, not justice of this world but Justice in the 'God' 'Universe', whatever word you use for 'the big Kahuna'.

On the way home from Sandy's my Dad and I were having a philosophical conversation. We were talking about Manifesting and our power in this world and how things work. We are both metaphysical, self-help book junkies. After spending two peaceful hours on Sandy's table I was in a Peaceful place. I calmly stated my current belief, that the cause is our beliefs (ultimately our desire, separation or connection) and this world is the effect. Let me make it clear that I don't believe we are willing to always look at all of our beliefs, so this is not always readily apparent to us.

I'm adding this paragraph in because I feel like in this journey I haven't properly addressed what I think was a pivotal moment. One of these hidden beliefs was shown to me in the Energy treatment that I had the day after diagnosis. In a distance, on the phone session, I was led to the 'root' of the issue. I saw myself being born, I hated it, it was cold and startling and I was crying and thinking, "get me out of here." It didn't stop there, as the practitioner gently led me forward I saw myself go back in and experience the birth again, with awareness, with warmth, with love and gentleness, you can imagine how powerful this was. I went back in a third time, this time into 'no expectancy," wide open, "baby your a firework" kind of place. This decision to 'stay here' was the beginning of healing.

This is not something that I need anyone to join me in, it's more of a set up on what I want to share.

Skip ahead to Wednesday, yesterday, I wrestled yesterday. I wrestled with a body that did not want to eat, a more intense gross taste in my mouth, fear of having to do this 6-8 more times, headaches, perpetual running nostrils and bloody nose, regret at having had the chemo., questioning whether having the chemo. was a denial in my faith in the healing power of God, or the body, or my belief system, all in all a real mind fuck. I tossed and turned, unable to rise for anything but going to the bathroom, I spent the past two days with Kleenex shoved up both nostrils (didn't post that picture, did I)!. I heard Dusty call my Mom and Dad and say that it was fine for them to take the kids to Cranbrook, I was glad. I reached out to a mentor and this is what she wrote:

"Chemo? Does is feel, "right" for you? Chemo has no meaning of its own...we give everything all the meaning it has for us. If using it temporarily gives you some peace, then use it! And while using it, give it to HS deep within asking for Him to show you what HE wants you to feel, to know and to remember. Pain or suffering is NOT God's Will...so you can claim your healing any moment that you are ready. The body has no ability to betray you...maybe you could take this thought to HS too and ask Him to demonstrate this if it feels right. Ultimately Fawna, you are perfect. Stay true to your Self. And listen. No effort. No struggle. Forgive the body for what it did not do. Sit with HS and together write it a Love letter...realizing that the body could never betray you...what would you say to it? And to Holy Spirit? What do you want to say to your Self? What desires to be brought to the LIGHT and transformed by it?

I am with you in this. We all are. Jesus is here. Atonement is done. All healing has already been accomplished in Jesus' Resurrection. Let's join Him now in our joint commitment to ACCEPT, to RECEIVE his Love and heal the guilt that used the body for attack.
With infinite Love,
Nouk xoxoxoxo"
Whoa, this feels like very deep sharing for me here. Many of you have commented on courage, this is the first time I am calling on Courage.
Trying to wrap the head around this doesn't work for me, I hear it in my gut, in the opening of my heart space. I hear the faint bell of truth on the outer limits of my awareness.
So this is where I sit today. I still didn't get out of bed, I feel good enough that I was tempted to, but this is such an opportunity to be quiet and have my thoughts revealed.
Today it was revealed to me that there is a thought in my mind about the 'glory of suffering', that it is okay to have what I want, but only if I purchase it with some suffering. This is guilt. It is okay for me to get out of the jobs that I don't really want if I have cancer, it is okay to lay in bed all day thinking about God, it is okay to tell everyone that I love them and its okay to receive their free and uncompromising love, if I'm sick. This tiny mad idea has some fairly unintended consequences.
A couple of months ago one of our boys at the Ranch (a great teacher) did something that he was not supposed to do. We were all scared for him, but we truly love and believe in this kid and it was a totally understandable mistake considering his age and background. I was called in to do some counselling with him and in the hour we spent together a great truth was illuminated. I knew that he was feeling particularly guilty about approaching a staff who he has a great relationship with, so that's where I took him. He said he was going to stay in the car, and when I said, "Are you sure?" he mustered up the courage to come in.

As he sat in a chair head down, facing away from this loving person, I saw myself, I saw myself with God. He wasn't looking at her so he couldn't see that she was not angry at all, she was relieved and happy to see him, and she assured him that she would always be there for him, but he wouldn't look to see it.

The other day I wrote on Facebook "Focusing on the Resurrection," that's where I'm at, having and giving the Love that I am without the pain, guilt and suffering, just letting it go. Forgiving you, forgiving me, actually having a good time here.

I'm feeling a bit of an urge to defend this 'belief' system, to talk about the 'Observer Effect' that has been proven in scientific experiments (haha, there, I just did it). Many of you have been calling me strong, our True strength is in defencelessness. I am laying aside fear and my need to defend or attack, I'm just opening up to your thoughts, feelings, ideas or nothing at all.

I assure you that I am feeling very healed in this moment. I don't know what is coming next but I'm grateful for the opportunity to step into this.

Love You.

Chapter 16
Bringing it All Together
4/15/12

The theme of this weekend was bringing it all together! For example, on my bedside right now there is:
A small bottle of Holy Water from Lourdes
Vick's Vaporub
Essiac Tea
Angel Cards
Tylenol Extra
Journal
A Course In Miracles
A Womens Study Bible
3 Andara Crystals, a Selenite and a Rose Quartz
An Interpretation of the Bhagavad Gita
Success Rituals 2.0 (featuring my friend Kim Page Gluckie)
Copy of "The Girl Who Played with Fire"
A hand painted picture from Thailand from my brother and sister in law
I AM WORD, Paul Selig (another book...)
Update- I am feeling calm, healthier than I have for months, hungry, and I can breathe through my left nostril (dreamy)I can talk clearly again and say the word 'bean'. I'm noticing that I feel a little protective not wanting to go into crowds or busyness, just enjoying the Peace of my house and moments with family and friends, online and in person.
I am not particularly great at any 'Left Brain Activities', enjoying movies over reading, quiet and listening to music. Hair intact, only a tiny bit of mouth soreness, so all in all it

feels miraculous. The shrinkage on the tumours is difficult to gauge, but where I had a large mass inside on the roof of my mouth, one on my neck, one near my left ear, in the left and right nostrils, now there is ONLY an inability to breathe through the right nostril and if I look deep with a flashlight I can see a faint pearly whiteness. This is compared to the complete filling and expansion of the right nostril with the tumour grossly visible.

Yesterday I spent two hours on my friends Crystal Healing Bed, we were both shocked, seemed like it had been an hour. Velva Dawn is an author, healer and just so much that I can't even list it here, please look her up. We have been treating each other on and off for years and we never know what to expect. She followed guidance and intuition and man oh man, it was Divine. I won't go into two hours of detail, but the overall theme seemed to be "Bring It All Together."

We both come from a medical science background and have been drawn into the 'woo-woo' :)

We talked about the value in just doing what is Guided (this discernment takes some self-awareness and practice) which included reflexology (something we are both trained in but use less than the 'energy' work). Even her iPod agreed with us, inserting a JLo dance tune in the midst of chants and healing tunes, and it was so perfect, the words were so right that they brought tears to my eyes!

I am following the diet as given, it is what I want to eat, so it's been easy, I am taking a few supplements and immune boosters and (possibly a relief for some of you to hear), anticipate having a second chemo treatment on April 30.

My thoughts on the chemo at this point, and I am willing to allow them to change, is to be mindful. If I become completely symptom free I want to be tested and see what's going on.

I just can't not mention here that my belief is that ALL of this healing is coming from the Mind, from the inside out and not the other way around, this brings a 'sameness' to the treatments.

The prayers, generosity in all of its forms (I will have to do a list at some point, it is REMARKABLE), and well wishes lift us all.

Dusty and I spent a great day in reflection today, he with his 15 pack and me with my tea, we talked about perspective and judgement and moving forward. We are being well cared for.

I'll close with what Jake (14yrs) just said to me "Mom, what if while the tumour was dying it screamed a little scream the whole time"- LOL- yeah, that would suck.

Chapter 17
You Matter
4/16/12

In my posts recently I may have talked about 'letting go' or 'going in' or 'undoing' and I have had some people expressing that, "Sometimes Fawna I have no idea what you are talking about."

I woke up at 4 am this morning with a concrete example of the process I am currently going through with this and want to share with you the last 20 minutes.

I woke up with the mind busy, as happens. I was watching how a post earlier in the evening, a post from a friend who's parents are separating showed the family sign where the woman's name has now been chiseled off was affecting me.

"What about this bugs me so much?" I am not alone, sometimes just putting it on someone else for a second so I can see it better works, I tried it out on my friend and on her Mom. "This feels significant" "Why is chiseling a name off seem like such a deep hurt, on some level it's just a sign, what does it matter?" PING, the word matter had a tiny 'hey there' quality. "It's like she's just been erased, like she just didn't matter."

At this point I can feel a truth feeling descend on me, an 'oops, there it is'.

So I take it home.

In my mind's eye I explore "You Don't Matter" and I feel the vague rumblings over the past few days, under the gratitude for your outpouring a faint "Why Me? It's too much? Strong?" A subtle minimizing of your overtures. I noticed the itchiness of "Why you are blogging anyway, are you just trying to get attention? Who really cares? Does it really matter?" I watch in my mind and see how there is indeed a tiny sliver of me that holds the belief, a part of me that while watching a friend who wants to kill herself this week say 'well, it doesn't really matter, life is eternal, there is no loss in the Universe', a spiritual truth in one way but in the feeling of it a dullness, a despair, a quality of 'meh-you live and then you die, that's the way it goes, IT DOESN'T REALLY MATTER."

So when this exploration feels complete I noticed in my body that there has been a tension in my back, running all the way from head to toe like a sheet. I have been attempting to fully, fully relax this week and this sheet remains.

Finally I make the decision that I am going to put this on the altar before Jesus (my own little visual that works for me, it changes from time to time). As I am moving towards the altar in my mind it feels like I have a sacred cow. "You Don't Matter" has a weight and a quality of 'my precious'. In my mind I place this before my loving companion, my confident, my friend Jesus and he smiles at me. I feel myself let the weight go and I rest in allowing Grace to take the residue from me and allow me to choose again.

I sit in "You Matter", I say it to myself over and over, feeling the tension lift, I say it in my head over and over until it morphs into "I Matter" as I begin to personalize it. I Matter.

This is not I matter in a world way, not in a "you matter to your kids, people rely on you, people need you" sort of way. This is the essence under that, You Matter just because, because you are part of all of this and for absolutely no reason at all, it just is, You Matter, I Matter.

Thanks, Love You

Chapter 18
Following Your Heart
4/18/12

I've been touched by the gifts I've been receiving, not so much for the material value, but I am finding that those around me are offering gifts of themselves. They are offering items that make them happy, they are extending their talents. This week has been a perfect example of this.

My friend Jane offered singing lessons ("I was in the bath and I was thinking it would be great for your throat and lungs") so watch for us on tour. There are too many to mention. Monday and Tuesday were perfect examples of how it all works out when you follow your heart.

On Monday we got the kids off to school and I realized I was a bit more fatigued than I thought. I puttered around the house a bit until the dog started going crazy, it was my friend Lee-Anne who is a wildlife photographer, she brought me the most beautiful picture of an eagle (the imagery of the eagle has been showing up a lot). Lee-Anne and I had tea and I was expecting Cara and Jager (a good friend of Gus) for lunch.

Cara arrived with Salad and Bubbles! Cara is full of energy, her enthusiasm for the bubbles was contagious. I am quite sure that I would not have ventured outside on Monday, let alone outside and play. As we ran around the yard I realized how fun and outdoors were also a critical part of this healing process. As I'd become ill over the winter I had been spending increasing time indoors, despite little pangs that going out for a walk would be a good thing to do. Not only did we get to play but there just so happens to be a photographer on hand, excited to shoot bubbles and play!

Cara was happy, I was happy, the boys were pure Joy and the photo's that Lee-Anne captured are magical. Before the day was out I was also given supper and cookies for the kids!

On Tuesday I ventured out on my own for the first time in a couple of weeks. This story needs to be told from the very beginning.

In running the Highwood River Inn this winter I was really interested in bringing events in that I was passionate about. This birthed some amazing house concerts and there are some fabulous retreats coming this summer. Alisa Gamblin, of Garden of the Mind Hypnotherapy in Nanton, and I decided it would be great to view and discuss some spiritual and expansive thinking films. We set this up for the spring and we were able to do one show, otherwise it just didn't fly. Instead of thinking this was a failure, here is how it was a total success. At the one event I met a lovely woman from Millarville, Deb Elliot. Deb was passionate about sharing a book and some work with me. She got my number and we met so that she could give me the book and tell me a little bit more about Brandon Bays-The Journey. It is fascinating work, Brandon healed herself from a basketball sized tumour. Now remember, this is before I knew I was sick! I used 'the Journey' work both before and after diagnosis and had some really great insights. Last week Deb sent me a note asking if I liked the book, I told her the whole story and commended her on following her heart and being so persistent in getting me the book, it was truly helpful. She offered to lead me through the process and as I am apt to do right now, I said, "yes."

So that's where I went Tuesday, to meet with Deb at her home and have her run me through "The Journey." All I had to do was sit and close my eyes and then she runs through 'a script' leading me back to where a healing is required. The experience was phenomenal, I'm not going to go through the details, but I came away feeling clearer, more centred and I am becoming increasingly convinced that WE are the light of the world.

The point of this, besides telling you how very lucky and magical my life has become, is that when you share the gift of your passion it is good for EVERYBODY. No sacrifice, no obligation, no loss.

Thank You to all of you who continue to share yourselves with me, I am truly grateful.

Chapter 18
I Heard the Little Scream
4/21/12

If you read one of my recent posts you will remember that my son Jake said, "Mom, What if the tumour screamed a little scream as it died?" Well, this week I heard the little scream, but it wasn't the tumour, it was 'helpful, helpful Fawna'. Like in the Wizard of Oz she was screaming "I'm melting, I'm melting."

I have had very clear prompts from the Holy Spirit that this is a time of Receiving and a chance to let go of some well worn patterns. Without guilt, without a belief that I've done something wrong. With the realization that much (not all) of my 'helping' came from disguised righteousness, lack of belief in other people or God, a Saviour Complex, a need to be seen as 'nice Fawna', all from the ego. Google "Jacuzzi lifeguard with Will Farrell and Jim Carey" and you will see what I'

So here's how it showed up this week, I've been being really good about not helping, when I don't feel good. When I had my treatment with Velva Dawn I was told that I am in a 'candy wrapper' and am not to come out until the time is right. On Wednesday I reached my little T-Rex arm out when a client from the Inn called "Fawna, You are the only one I can trust", good one ego! By the end of the day I was exhausted and all of those who've been guarding me were pissed right off!

That night I had a dream with the same theme, my cousin 'needed' me and it was crucial, it was 50% of her mark! In the dream we were both stressed right out.

I woke up in the morning and heard the little scream. One of my spiritual mentors said to me a few weeks ago, "What parts are you not going to salvage, are you not going to save, this is an opportunity to step out of the 'character' of Fawna."

So this begs the question, "Isn't it good to help?", of course it is, in the movie "Happy" by Tom Shadyac he talks about helping as one of the most helpful steps towards happiness. What I'm talking about is letting go of the helping with strings, the kind that leads you to resentment, or the manipulative helping, the helping that is to prevent conflict or criticism (hmm...that's me).

Many times I've said to my clients, if you are a helper you cannot and will not stop helping, it's about putting yourself in the mix. So I guess the truth is - I'm not stopping helping (I LOVE helping), I'm helping myself right now.

I know there have been times in my life where my closest circle is exasperated with me, my parents will recognize my need to rest and they will take the kids and while they are gone I will go and help someone move, or sit with a depressed friend.

The actions are not wrong in any way, actions are neutral. I'm asking myself, "What Is behind This?" "Why am I doing this?" "Is this an Obligation or a Heart Desire?" "Ego or Highest Self?"

Self-Awareness means taking a look at every action, every thought, every reaction, "Why?" I want to be a teacher of light, love and wholeness, I no longer desire to feed the pain and suffering that keeps the idea of Separation going.

Chapter 19
Focusing on the Gifts
5/6/12

We have been without internet for a week so it was a chance to unplug (aka torture the teens).
Where I'm at right now is a week after the second chemotherapy. I met with my lovely team, 2 doctors and a nurse at Tom Baker on April 27 to get the low down on their plan. They were thrilled with the results of the initial treatment and how I was feeling. In a short visit they lined out their plan to treat this as a 'new' occurrence and therefore take least invasive measures first (yay)! Three sessions of RCHOP (chemotherapy) followed by a PET scan and radiology consult. I was thrilled, 2 more sessions, easy peasy!
Over the time since the first chemotherapy I continued to accept offers of supplemental treatments, I had a Reiki + session with Sandy Day from High River. I made a commitment to see Sandy for her nurturing treatments monthly in 2005, in May that year I became miraculously pregnant with Gus. I had been told that I would NOT become pregnant after the Stem Cell Transplant and had in menopause for years. Sandy is where I go when I want to feel complete unconditional love and attention.
The second week I had a "Journey" session with Deb Elliot from Millarville, this was a profound session, uncovering beliefs about being 'let down' by 'spiritual teachers', being betrayed, not being trusted and not trusting. In uncovering these I am able to choose again, to choose to trust and heal. I have had several people say, "I couldn't do that, I'm not that in tune", it's just not true, there is an element of fear in

looking at these beliefs and a stronger relief when you have the courage to do so. The power of these sessions are that they take you right to your Source, to your Truth and allow you to access that Wisdom- all in a couple of hours of guided meditation.

In the final 'rest' week I had a massage/Cranial-Sacral treatment and Oxygen therapy with Sheila Harvey at the beautiful Chimney Rock Wellness Retreat.

I have continued to receive distance healing from yoga groups, drum groups, healers and prayer circles from everywhere.

The moral support on Facebook and in email has been remarkable, people reaching out with their love and their own stories.

I finished reading Wayne Dyer's "Wishes Fulfilled" and Anita Moorjani's "Dying To Be Me."

After waking drowned in hair last Sunday Dusty insisted on shaving my head, I let it go too far to do the mullet or Mohawk! It's been a week and for goodness sake it is growing! Gus found it scary at first and then enjoyed scaring his friends with it (my bald head) this week.

Chemotherapy last Monday was much quicker, I spent a couple of hours sleeping through it and just managed it much better this past week. I took all the medications I was supposed to and did my best to truly rest (realizing this is not my strong suit). The chemotherapy leaves me feeling hungover, tired, gross taste in the mouth and nauseated however, after months of feeling miserable I would say that overall I am feeling better. By Thursday I was well enough to take the 3 kids shopping and go to Costco. I saw Sandy Day again and today was treated to a visit and a Crystal Healing Kit from Grace Diamond.

I continue to wake in the middle of the night with meditation and insights. This week is what about eliminating dis-ease, and my desire to remove all barriers to Ease. Ease in relationships, ease in support, ease in health, in every area. I saw how the current situation is a chance to grind to a halt. A chance to redirect towards heart centered living, a chance to stop 'trying' to be perfect and accept my perfection, as is, here and now. I also have a strong sense that all of this is happening through me, not by me, that Grace is acting on me in a way that is NOT under personal control and that there is a sense of evolution to it, it's just time. Time to give up one way of living for another. Without judgement on the past or on what 'other' people are doing.

What this adds up to is GRATITUDE. I continue to allow myself to Love and Be Loved - allowing pieces of dis-ease with this to fall away. I have had miraculous support all around me, from my husband and kids to our accountant, lawyer and banker (seriously)! And everyone in between.

This weekend I booked flights to New Mexico to join the Power of Power Retreat. I will step away from my life for a week and I look forward to the opportunity to step away from old roles, Mom, Wife, Daughter as well as this recent role of 'cancer person'. I look forward to listening and hearing.

I don't have a point today, sharing more than anything, sharing all of it.

Dusty and I have both been struck by our 'fear detector', the room when we left chemotherapy on Monday was FULL of it, heavy, choking fear and despair. Dusty mentioned 'they should have comedians in here'. The loss of hair seems to trigger people, both of us feeling their terror as a discordant hum. This hits us mostly as a surprise as we are not in a space of 'Fawna is dying' and so when we see it sets us back, Dusty usually starts to laugh, it doesn't seem to last long when people tune in.

I'm grateful for all of you who are following and participating in this journey, we are in this together and I invite you to love yourself with me. I'd really like to hear some response from some of you for what's going on with you too, share your insights, your growth, your miracles.

In Peace,

Fawna

In between my second and third chemotherapy treatments I chose to fly to Sante Fe and go on retreat. This required putting my chemotherapy off a week, making the treatment my own has taken some time and courage. We are conditioned to listen to your doctors, they know best. This change was easy and unquestioned and just felt right.

It was a wonderful break. With my bald head covered in the silk scarves that I had bought to teach and treat the chakra's I ended up in Sante Fe all alone at 2 am. I had chosen the cheapest hotel I could find and booked online. At 2 am this did not seem like the best choice. The girl at the hotel was locked in a room behind glass and set my key through a small opening, this didn't help my rising level of anxiety, I then followed down the hall, out of the lights into the darkened back corner to my room. I was thinking that if my Mom and Dad knew, they would kill me. My heart beat quickly and my hands were a little shaky as I put the key in the door and rushed into the room quickly closing the door. By the light of day it was far less menacing. Through all of this I continued my practice of watching all of these feelings, seeing where I was scared, where the urge to protect the body showed up. I spent the next day wandering the shops of Sante Fe, with my rolly suitcase, had a wonderful breakfast on my own and made my way to meet the transport to the monastery where the retreat was being held. Two women sat with their luggage waiting, one from New Jersey and one from California. We chatted easily, knowing that we were going to the same place. It was a tiny thrill when a fully robed monk, beige, full length robes, picked us up for the drive to Peco's. Brother Anthony was a joy, recalling his story of moving from millionaire in his early 20's to complete loss and homelessness to his call from God. Despite being obviously devoutly Catholic there were amazing parallels in our beliefs and callings, in our truths'. The monastery at Peco's was an old dude ranch, a rambling old adobe and timber building with small, simple bedrooms, a large eating area and a gorgeous chapel, complete with bells. It is located on the banks of a small river and surrounded by large willows and other trees, the green standing out against the high desert red rocks of Peco's. It was fantastical. The monks, the quiet, the pictures of Jesus and the statues of Mother Mary thrilled me to the core. Other participants in the workshop, who had deep issues with the Catholic church, were not as thrilled, placing Jesus in their drawers and feeling tension in the restrictions of the space. Meals were primarily silent and we dined with the monks. The workshop itself was like a major confirmation for me, I have loved A Course In Miracles for some time and at the same time LOVED my energy and body work. In some circles these are seen as conflicting idea's. Here in this space Nouk, Stacy and Carrie were bringing them all together. I had a private session with Stacy and dropped right into the Christ consciousness, what alarmed me was that it felt completely normal, with a lack of 'excitement' but a depth of peace and stillness and is-ness. This is becoming increasingly stabilized as time goes by, but by no means a constant feeling.

The other participants were an alarmingly varied group, in age, background and personality. Despite this there was an immediate comradery and an exercise that involved hugging to John Lennon's showed up on the first day (apparently this was usually an end of the week activity). I was in my element. The funniest part of the week was when, near the end of the week, after mentioning that I had cancer (I had chosen not to talk about it, take a break) one woman shared that she had no idea I had cancer and that she had thought I was a French Nun. After a week of meditating and talking about God I was in a trusting and happy space, I did not have a room booked for the night I went back and on the last day the girl next to me turned and asked if I needed a room, she had one booked that we could share. She and I spent the day in Sante Fe together and the evening in joy with other classmates.

Despite being virtual strangers there was not a feeling of discomfort and after a week in near silence we seemed to have lots to talk about. This connected feeling continued as I got on a shuttle to the airport. I spent the entire drive speaking with a 22 year old artist from Detroit sharing our deepest thoughts and beliefs with ease.

I came home refreshed, lucky for me as some more drama had unfolded. It is touched on in this blog.

Chapter 20
Pause, Rewind, Fast Forward
5/28/12

It's been a little bit since I blogged and I've been getting word that a few of you are worried. May need to get a live cam, reality show type crew to follow me, your worry on me is wasted. I am happy as a clam. Today, I noticed that I was completely content; I was doing my taxes, I have chemo tomorrow and a PET scan on Wednesday and I was as happy as I was in Pecos, NM on retreat.

I stepped out of my 'regular' life for a week in a Monastery in New Mexico on a retreat with teachers Nouk Sanchez, Carrie Triffet and Stacy Sully. Their teachings are based on A Course In Miracles, a text who's main tenants are making the choice between Faith and Fear and using Forgiveness as a tool to invite Peace, Love and Harmony into your life. These gentle and humble teachers invited an honest look at our thinking and gave us the tools to 'let go' and to 'embody' the Miracle Maker. Thanks to the loving support of Dusty, the kids and our families I was able to completely immerse myself in the quiet time and the connection to Spirit, I can't think of a nicer gift. Taking the time to stop and go within (Pause) allows me to see the 'crazy making' thoughts that are ever present (Rewind) and then to shoot closer to the awareness that I Am Love. This sense has begun to fill me, warming me and drawing me closer to everyone, friends, family and beautiful strangers on the shuttle.

This presence was welcomed as I returned to hear that my sister in laws parents, long time neighbours had been in a head on collision and were fighting for their lives. As with the story of cancer, this is a shared experience, felt deeply by a wide circle and weighing heavily on those closest to the family. My brother and sister in law (not the same one) were the first on scene and handled it unbelievably well, but were understandably shaken.

The overwhelming sense that I have is that we are all in this together, that in sharing our vulnerability we show that we no longer need the strong defenses, the walls, the misguided controlling behaviours that keep us separate. Our connection is our strength.

So, if you are wondering how I am, I have to say better than ever. I'm in a space where the words are not quite enough, so I ask you to stop now, close your eyes and drop your awareness into your body, the heart, the belly, drop in, tune in and join me in the openness here. I ask you to feel how I'm feeling, and I assure you that you will not be worried any more.

Love You!

The third chemo was completely uneventful and with few side effects, less than round one and two.

Dusty and I continued with our great hospital vibe falling into a companionable silence and feeling like we were far happier than anyone else in the space.

Here is the most popular blog I wrote about this second cancer journey.

Chapter 21
How is Dusty Doing?
5/29/12

A few weeks ago I began to get asked "How is Dusty Doing?" again and again. I asked him if he would do a blog, or tell me and I would post it. He obliged, and I remember his entire blog word for word:

"How the Fuck do you think I am?" Dusty Bews

I was thinking that would have a strong appeal to my family who all profess to have ADD (and have noted that my blogs are too long).
I have laughed about his statement over and over. That's how it is with Dusty, he makes me laugh because he says things that I may have thought but don't think to say.
Dusty has been a rock. He knocked it out of the park 12 years ago, proving that he took the "In sickness and in health" promise seriously. He remembers every med and blood count and detail, allowing me to float in my rainbow haze loving everyone.
He was with me when I was diagnosed, I went to "Shit I have to tell everyone" and he went to "Fuck, I don't want to have to watch you go through this again." Once we got over this we are united in knowing that I will get through this better than anyone can believe, laughing at all the dark humour that emerges in the situation and stepping up to the task of helping manage me, the kids and our life, while still working 40+ hours per week.

Dusty does not allow me to wallow in self-pity, giving 'to the point advice' as needed "If you would get off of your ass you would feel better." I am grateful that we have some wonderful friends and our parents that he can lean on.

When we went through this in 2000 he quit work (was working on the movie "The Claim" at Fortress) and was with me every step of the way, doing puzzles, remembering and watching me. He just told me that he doesn't do puzzles this time. Over the years I've often thought that that time was harder on him than me. I remember saying, "Geez Dusty, when's the bad part, I feel great,

"He said, "Honey, you are as high as a kite." I'm sure you all get it- and hence the question "how is Dusty doing?"

Now don't get me wrong, he's not ready for sainthood yet, his bickering with our 13 year old makes me want to tear out my itty bitty hairs.

In my opinion Dusty is doing great, he is here, he is supportive, he is understanding and he is fun. I feel lucky.

Here is the Mother's Day gift that Dusty made me, a raised garden (planted on Sunday with the help of my friend Suzi).

Chapter 22
From. Afar.
5/29/12

I am smiling and jumping with excitement to share a note from my friend Tia. As I wrote to Tia, thank you for giving helplessness a voice, I know that this will be helpful.
This is a shared experience and if we can be open to every voice we will have an amazing choir, that's what I want.
Embrace it all, no man (woman) (transgendered/neutral) left behind.
Thank You, Thank You, Thank You Tia. When this is over we will go out for lobster.
"Hi Beautiful ... I cannot stop thinking about you. I stole your blog title and wrote...
I'm sorry if the obscenities offend ... I wanted you to know.
Everyday Aha: From. Afar.
As I sit and reread Fawna's blogs for the millionth time, feeling like a stalker monitoring her page, I am struck by the "somethings" that are stirring inside me. Okay, not stirring, but like my six-year old says, "Mommy, it feels like there is a lobster in my tummy that keeps snapping its pinchers inside me. It hurts. I don't know if I'm mad or sad or worried." So, for some unknown reason, I feel compelled to blog (not that I have my own) about these "lobsters" in my tummy whenever I creep Fawna's page for an update.
"Everyday Aha: From Afar" – this title guides my writing at this very moment. The internet tab on my computer which reads "FaceBook" is something that I click on every ten

minutes with Fawna's page just to see if there is an update. This all started about two weeks ago when my BlackBerry lost every piece of data I had in it and none of it was recoverable. I sent out a mass email for my contacts (of which Fawna was one) to send me their information again. As always, Fawna is the "first on the scene" and responded within mere moments to my "distress" – giving me every phone number that she thought I might need. I texted her later that week – suggesting coffee – with her replying that when she returned from her retreat, it was a plan in the works. Because Fawna seems to always be on these self-discovery retreats, I went on her FaceBook page to see what she was up to this time ... thinking maybe she was learning some new skill with those rocks that people use for massage, some new meditation technique or a new idea for helping people ...
I cried. From. Afar.
Since then, I have thought about Fawna every day – almost every hour of every day ... I'm sure her loved ones think about her every millisecond of everyday ... and those "somethings" just won't stop going ... damn lobsters. In an effort to put it out there "From Afar" and after being inspired by Dusty's Blog: "How the Fuck do you think I'm doing," I thought maybe it was time to share thoughts. From. Afar.
I don't intend to make this blog about me but hopefully, some of these words are echoed by others. From. Afar.
Here we go ... From. Afar. I think:
1. Really?!?! Again?!?! What the FUCK?!?!
Cancer? Yes, you! You are an asshole.
2. Fucking Bring IT!!!
Cancer? You chose the wrong lady. You are evil and bad and unfortunately for you – you are going to get your ass kicked again ... I'm all for watching you shrink and shrivel. For the benefit of us all, go the FUCK away quickly ... and stay gone. A'right?
3. Pick on Someone Else!

Can't you see, Cancer? Fawna is NEEDED, LOVED, ESSENTIAL and BEAUTIFUL!! She is everything you aren't. You sneak the fuck up on people ... impose yourself where you aren't wanted and on the people that deserve (not that anyone does) you the LEAST. Hear me? Fuck off!

4. What does one say? From. Afar?
As a social worker for two decades, I am supposed to figure out the words that have meaning and are appropriate and make things "better". It's like wanting to put on a band-aid, buy a big fucking lollipop and a pony to make it all "okay". I cannot. I cannot make it better (meaning make the cancer go away), I cannot find the words to tell Fawna how it feels to see her body hurting (From.Afar), I cannot find the logic to understand when Fawna tell us everything is okay, that she feels good, that she is peaceful and happy and not want to yell out loud - obscenities! From. Afar.

5. Is Fawna really okay? From. Afar?
I have the qualitative opportunity to know Fawna and her family over the years – although quantitatively, have not had the time that lots of others have spent with her. Fawna, the epitome of grace, kindness, love and "putting everyone else before herself", would tell everyone that she is okay. But is she really? That's my question and I may not have the context that others have to accurately know. From. Afar. I search her pictures, her eyes, wonder what her thoughts are when she is alone ... and wonder if she is really okay? Really? Okay? Truth be known, I think she might be doing better than the rest of us.

6. There are NO other options. From. Close. And. Afar.
There are no options. Just like there weren't when Fawna first battled this demon. If anyone in this world has the spirit and love to overtake this beast, it's Fawna. She is love ... LOVE ... and there is nothing else more powerful in this world to erase the bad ... all of us combined, there is NO other option.

7. All of my Wishes. From. Afar.

Fawna? You have all of my wishes, my hopes and my most pleading prayers that I've saved up and never used. You have all of my dreams that I missed wishing on that falling star ... you have my warmest of hugs, my most pleading and hoping of tears, my respect, my admiration for your strength and grace ... and all of the blessing that the Grandfather's and God will bring.

Love. From. Afar.
Tia"

Tia's feelings summed up a lot of the feelings of the people around me. Getting them to believe that I'm okay continues today- 7 months after treatment. Some of my closest friends expressed extreme distress at diagnosis, crying for days, and feeling alienated by my new beliefs and all of my healer friends, feeling helpless and hopeless and that I had somehow left them for a different life. I have no words but truth for these friends, look inside, trust me, look after yourself and know that I am at peace and when I'm not I know how to get there.

Chapter 22
Deserve?
6/8/12

A friend asked if I pre-write my blogs. It seems like they 'percolate', bubbling up until all of a sudden they are ready to be written.
Yesterday I had the prompt that this one was READY!
The prompt was a Facebook comment. I had gone on an overnight retreat Tuesday and had outlined what a great time it was, one of my friends commented "Well deserved..."

About a month ago my husband mentioned that he didn't think the kids 'deserved' lunch money. The reaction that I had was confusion, what does that even mean?
It seems that we have set up an economy of deserved ness. Depending on how much you suffer, you will be given your allotment of nice. The amount will be in direct correlation to how much you believe you are worth, with extra credit to you if you have some sort of pain, struggle or victim hood.
The amount will be completely arbitrary depending on the person, and I'm noticing that most people think someone else's suffering is worse than their own. Unless of course they have denied themselves long enough to hit "what about me????"
Can you see how this economy is self-perpetuating and keeps us in a cycle of suffering punctuated by small oasis of happy or good or nurturing?
How often do we justify meeting our own needs over another's needs because of this concept "this will hurt them,

but dammit, I deserve it." I don't have a problem with this except for because we are One, any acts of separation will ultimately feed guilt, keeping the whole machine in perpetual motion.

We have elevated cancer to the realm of awful where you deserve everything! We were cracking up at a golf tournament when I revealed my bald head and 'puss in boots' face to be the next table up to the buffet.

When I meditate on Deserve I find no such idea in Love. Or another way to look at it, an all-encompassing idea, All deserving all!

All deserving All? It's so foreign to this world that the mind goes, what? Crazy talk Fawna- that can't work?

The concept of punishment and reward is deeply embedded. I'm only suggesting 'what if?'.

What if you deserve to be happy as a birthright? What if you stopped denying yourself or your people dependent on perceived worth? What if we trusted that our needs and others would be met without our continual interference in the form of "this is fair and this is not fair" that is handed out from a very limited space of awareness. Wow- longest sentence ever! What I'm saying is, we don't have the big picture- on our selves or anyone else, we can agree on that, right? Yet we continually think that we know who deserves what, and how much. The formula is complicated and unique dependent on how you were raised, no wonder we disagree so much!

Continually on this journey I've caught myself going to turn the tap of receiving down - or off- "okay- that's enough- a week in Santa Fe, stop the good for a while- you have your cup full". We all know that person "no, I'm good, I'm fine, that's enough." That's enough? Says who? How do you know?

Have you ever had that sense that when things are going great that there is some form of payment lurking in the background? Some sort of suffering will need to balance out this goodness. I know a lot of us with healthy kids live with this "I have so much- what's gonna happen?" Some of us will self-limit in the hopes of preventing having to 'pay' for good.

And of course there are the the ones who never have enough! This reminds me that in Truth we want Love- no other commodity can replace it.

We all deserve Love, all of it, tap wide open. It's the only currency that multiplies as we give or receive it. The retreats, gifts, goodies of this world are stand ins. It is a process though, accepting the good here is a way to start embodying your self-worth.

We have laughed several times over the past few months about my "get out of jail free card".

My process over the last few months has been a giving control over to God (the Universe, consciousness, whatever you call it). This idea of deciding/knowing who deserves what- both suffering and joy, seems to be one that has so many unintended consequences when I think I am qualified to be the judge.

One way to help with this process is appreciation, I love how this is also a word we use for growing money. When we appreciate receiving we seem to avoid thoughts of too much or not enough. Truly grateful for this forum to share thoughts!

I think that's all I have to say about that...

Love

Chapter 23
Shaken, Not Stirred
6/23/12

Two weeks ago I got the great news that my PET scan was negative. I've had a lot of people ask, so briefly, a PET scan shows metabolic activity, they show cells that consume sugar for energy, a negative indicates that there is not 'life' where there shouldn't't be. Great News!
In the same breathe I was told that we would be quickly beginning radiation. This would require cleaning up any dental problems that have the potential for becoming infected.
After a peaceful morning, Dusty and I in conversation and much laughing while we waited for the doctor I left the office shaky. I was crabby and couldn't wait to get somewhere and have a drink. My legs were literally weak and I felt off balance.
The image I have in my head is a jar of oil and water, where I had been in quite a still place where the two substances, or mindsets, love and fear, had been settled, separated and easy to see, for whatever reason (I'd like to blame radiation and dentistry but I know that the shaking comes from the inside not the outside), the jar was completely shaken and I've spent the past two weeks shifting between love and fear. Since my goal is to live in Love this is not a bad thing, I want to be shaken so I can see what's in there. It's like a background program running on your computer.
So, what this looks like is two weeks of wrestling. I know that to settle I need stillness, fear however has two reactions, fight or flight, definitely not stillness. Despite hearing the gentle

wisdom inviting me inwards I often chose to stay busy or irritated. No guilt, just noticing. Finally, three days ago I sat still in the morning, committing to alignment with Love, allowing that to fill me up. Ahhhh-the days slow down, irritation subsides and opportunities open up.

My process with the fear is not to cover it up or affirm it away as I've said before this is a bit like putting a fancy blanket on a dog poo. The dog poo is still there, stinking and never completely hidden. If I'm in fear of any kind (irritation, anger, sadness). Then I know I'm choosing to believe something that's not True. In the past two weeks I've uncovered mistaken beliefs in the 'value' of money, the power(?) of the body, viruses, infections, radiation and the concept of torturing/being tortured. My two and a half hour dentist appointment was a roller coaster, mind watching and releasing that reminded me of cleaning our junk drawer, stuff in there that I didn't realize!

It's been a bit like living in a split screen where I can see how the ego (fear) would have had me just suffering nonstop with sad stories and poor me's as opposed to gratitude and 'bring it on', 'let it rip!'.

I don't know if this makes any sense, but it's what makes the question "how are you?" difficult. On the physical, I'm doing great. The last chemo I had hardly any side effects. Mentally/emotionally I've been shaken but that's okay, and spiritually? Better than ever.

I have to mention here that some people found the mask pictures disturbing, my Mom says I should let you know that I had the Best time there. The two radiation therapists and I laughed and visited for 40 minutes.., the back of the mask is a foam that warms and expands around your head and neck and the front is warm and meshy, not hard to breathe at all. It was spa-like and 90% less uncomfortable than most beauty treatments (definitely nicer than a Brazilian wax)!

I am going into 20 treatments of radiation feeling clearer every day, divine guidance and my doctor agree that this is happening. I have no idea why, but that is part of the fun.

Living in the Mystery, stop pretending that I 'know' why, what, trusting that I'm loved and supported. Even with these blogs, I'm writing without planning or editing and the response has been gorgeous. I am completely reinforced that living without being guarded, without hiding things (to the degree that I'm able) leads to Miracles and connection.
Feeling it all,
Fawna

Chapter 24
Trying Peace vs. Peace
7/6/12

Two teeth pulled and 3 temporary fillings. This was just the tip of the iceberg in terms of the dental work I am potentially facing. Obviously there has been a reluctance to visit these professionals for some time, reluctance in this case is a major understatement. To be perfectly honest I was hoping for a Miracle healing, I even googled it, "Healing Teeth with the Mind." I believe that Shirley MaClaine may have done it.

The truth is, tooth work is relatively benign, particularly in this day and age of numbing and sedation. There seemed however to be no way to move this information from my brain to my body. My body in the dentist chair would seem to become seized with anxiety, a vibrating mass of concrete. I would feel tortured with a hangover of intense freezing that would seem to come on when I got into my car after the appointment.
I would often lament "My teeth are fine until I go to the dentist" and - "I believe in Fairies but I don't believe in Dentists."
I am smiling as I write this.
Over the past 12 years I have been intensely reading, reading to figure this whole shit show out. I continue to resonate with similar themes, themes of personal responsibility, the power of the mind and the Grace within each one of us. Many paths preach these idea's. So it is with these eye's that I look at the current situation.

As I shared in the last post the idea's of radiation and dentistry rocked my boat. During the 2 and 1/2 hour dental examination (required for preparation of radiation) I experienced a roller coaster of thoughts, emotions and beliefs, finding myself mistakenly identified as the torturer and the tortured.

So, how did the actual treatment go? I was sharing with a friend that during the treatment (as mentioned in the first sentence) I noticed the difference between trying to be peaceful and Being Peaceful. She said I should write that down, so here I am.

As I sat in the chair I could feel the familiar heart racing, this was confirmed by the dentist "is your heart rate always this high?" as the computer showed it at 99 beats per minute. With some deep breathing I was able to calm this somewhat.

What I believe may be helpful is the internal dialogue. It feels important to state here that there has been an 'impersonal' element to this entire situation over the past few months. This is not 'my' cancer, 'my' cancer treatment nor 'my' dentistry. I have not tried to cultivate an impersonal feel to it, that is just how it feels and that is why it's been easy to share with you. I don't know what any of this is for, despite the vast number of theories that my analyzing (anal-yzing as my friend Tomas would say) mind would like to put forth.

So my internal dialogue is full of idea's from A Course In Miracles, The Bible, The 4 Agreements, The Power of Now and Loving What Is, books that resonate and speak to me even before I could put their ideas into action.

Back to the chair. I lay there encouraging my body to relax, noticing everything, grounding (a process of bringing awareness to my feet, growing roots out, bringing myself completely into the body). Fears of pain and loss of control began to show up and in response I said (inside) "I am not upset for the reason that I think (the dentist) where is this coming from?" Backing it up I notice that I am not feeling safe and I follow, I know that thoughts precede feelings and that beliefs precede thoughts. I believe that I am not safe, I believe that I am this small body that can be harmed, I believe that this dentist is outside of me and a threat to me, when I am meditating I sit longer with these kind of beliefs, agreeing to disagree, remembering who I am and handing them over (to Jesus usually for me) and choose again. I shortcut as I'm in the chair and they are starting treatment- I am safe, I am loved, the dentist has only my best in mind for me. I find these affirmations most helpful only after uncovering what is causing my discomfort. When I try to use them to cover the panic without looking at it, well, I can hear the 'bullshit' right behind each affirmation, not as helpful.

As they settle in, quickly, no time between freezing and work and yet fully frozen, my mantra switches to "there is no problem here," this is a fairly recent addition, switching me from looking at what is wrong to settling into the 'is'. I also remind myself that all I jwant is Peace of mind (in the past I believe I wanted "get this over as soon as possible"). In this time I am also talking to my teeth. Thank You for what you have done, you are going to be taken out, this is for the highest good- and a voice comes in, a voice of one of my spiritual teachers, "You take these teeth very seriously" and I lighten out of giving too much to the teeth but feeling good about the acknowledgment nonetheless.

All of this is helpful, the relaxation, the mantra's, the mind watching and then,bam, GRACE. Oh, what a difference, suddenly, from within, welling up like a spring emerges from the earth - Peace and Calm. Peace and Calm without trying, peace and calm filling me, sending me into a space that is bigger than my body, feeling the sameness between the dentist, hygienist and myself. In this space my eyes feel heavy and instead of panic I almost feel like I could fall asleep while the dentist is dismantling my broken teeth and efforting them out! I am aware of a spaciousness inside and it is all okay. I still feel the pressure of the dentist exertion, I am aware of him saying, "You are doing so well". At this point I have a coughing fit, this too is no problem, we all take a break and I continue to sit peacefully, not trying to do anything, not trying to quit coughing or tough it out. We settle back in and the last piece pops out. We are done in an hour.

As I write this I feel that same feeling popping in, I would love to hear if you feel it too. I am impelled to write and publish this before we head out to the Calgary Stampede. Peace and Calm. Fawna

After chemo and before radiation, after the extractions we entered a celebratory time. Dusty and I went to a big party for the Calgary Stampede, I wore blue hair, a saucy dress and cowboy boots and danced all night (as did Dusty, but that's for his book), we went to the rodeo and to a 4 day weekend at the lake with my University friends. I'm sure I was tired, but I sure don't remember holding back very much.

Before Radiation there was the preparation. I had planned to bring Janet along to shoot pictures. I was completely surprised when, during a routine visit I was rerouted for the building of the mask. My mom and several friends were completely unprepared for these pictures and again painted a much different story than the truth. The truth was that this was another excellent adventure with two amazing men. In the basement of the hospital, where it seems many of these lovely souls are stored, I found two 'mask making' technicians. Obviously highly intelligent they reminded me of the guys from 'Big Bang Theory'. I explained my blog and my desire to have pictures and they showed intense desire to get the perfect shots for me. I lay my head into this base and it was gorgeously warm, then they placed the wet netting over my face, also warm and comfortable, honestly it was like a spa treatment! We laughed and enjoyed one another and the mask was born.

Chapter 25
How Do You Stay So Strong?
7/28/12

A couple of weeks ago during a rousing game of 'Scramble with friends', a friend asked "How Do You Stay So Strong?" This question has been bouncing around ever since.
I have ruminated on this question, chewed it up like cud and moved it through my four stomachs.
My initial response was more questions-
"Am I being strong?"
"What is strong?"
"Who is NOT being strong?"
And a statement:
"God is my strength", but what does that mean?
I saw a kitty poster (which I can't find for the life of me) that said, "Fear shared is cut in half", which made me think of the support group I have and how Fear cut into 1000 or more is nearly nothing.
Sharing has definitely strengthened me, sharing without expectations and without editing. At some level the biggest fear is that we are alone, separate; and by sharing, this lie just can't live.
As I shared about my dental fears I was overwhelmed by the number of others hiding what had been a secret shame of mine, as I shared about cancer I received gifts of the heart from all around, no matter what the form it said, "We are in this together."

I have been called strong when I admit that I'm having a hard day, and when I exclaim that everything is perfect, so it's not at all about the outside.

I have been moved by the fact that so many of us see strength in others while minimizing our own. Case in point, the person who asked me this question found out that the numbness in her legs was an inoperable tumour the very next day, and yet she keeps on trying to beat me at Scramble :). I have had letters from people who call me inspiring- and they themselves are going through battles that I would prefer not to. The fact is, we are all strong.

When do I feel strong, that is where God comes in. When I remember that I am an eternal spirit, invulnerable and limitless, well, strength just is. When I believe that I am a small body at the risk of danger/injury/hardship/hurt feelings at any moment, I'm scared, not just with cancer, but always!

I looked up Strong and this is the definition that fits best: "Not easily upset; resistant to harmful or unpleasant influences." Hopefully, she didn't mean this one " having an unpleasantly powerful taste or smell" maybe should have checked that.

I vacillate between not being easily upset and being easily upset but then looking into the WHY of it, this is where I'm finding gold. Instead of putting up with a life of one upset after another I truly believe that we need not suffer, it's supposed to be fun here!!!!!! As I erase the lies and the unwanted and limiting beliefs with forgiveness and shining the light on them I feel freer and less and less blown about by the ever changing winds of this world.

As I've said in other posts, I've chosen to have the strength to look at my crap this time, being aware of what I feel, what I'm thinking, what beliefs that that indicates and then decide whether that is where I want to keep operating from or not.

When I choose that Love is my ONLY purpose, it doesn't't matter what I'm seemingly going through, who I'm with, where I am. This is the only action I'm focusing on right now, trusting that the rest will fall into place (and it seems to be)!

I'm not sure that I 'stay' strong, but as all of you have shown me, when I show what this world calls weakness, well, that is seen as strong too!

In a nutshell
1. Sharing
2. Self Awareness
3. Honest Expression
4. Ask for Help (from God and the gods and goddesses around you).

AND finally, the answer I usually use:
"What else are we supposed to do?"

From ACIM Lesson 91

"I am not weak, but strong."
"I am not helpless, but all powerful."
"I am not limited, but unlimited."
"I am not doubtful, but certain."
"I am not an illusion, but a reality."
"I cannot see in darkness, but in light."

Chapter 26
Fawna, Clean Your Room!!!
7/9/12

Thought I had my computer but I don't, I'll get to do this blog from my iPhone! Catching inspiration as it strikes.

I've been mulling over how to share the difference in my approach to cancer last time and this time, on the outside it may look very similar, on the inside a little different.

On my way home from radiation I saw a helpful metaphor in my mind.

I saw the Febreze commercial

http://www.youtube.com/watch?v=TpB_MfhSreM&feature=youtube_gdata_player

The rooms are my mind, Febreze the tools I've accumulated (angels, affirmations, reframing, etc.).

I've collected tools- and they work. Instead of sitting in a filthy stinking room I am able to bring myself to a better, fresher smelling place. This is what I accomplished 12 years ago. Relative peace. This was peppered with the occasional deeply peaceful, Grace filled moments for sure, but generally it was a kind of 'good suffering'. There is no judgement here, only an awareness.

This time I have the tools to clean the room up. Continuing to use the Febreze over and over works, but ensures ups and downs, I would wait for the stink and then, squirt, squirt. Lately I've been questioning the logic of sayings like "if I didn't know pain how would I know joy," or "no rain, no rainbows." While these give us hope that this too will pass it also offers an acceptance, even a glory, in putting up with pain and suffering.

I am not saying we need to put all of our tools away, no, I'd rather clean in a pleasant atmosphere. I don't think we need to dive into the filth, roll around in it, and neither can we remain blindfolded and get it cleaned up.

The Living Miracles Church refers to it as 'ghosting' and I'm sure you've had the experience of feeling a bit of pain, worry, anger and quickly using whatever you have to quiet it down, whether it be a crystal, a rye and coke, counseling technique or a spiritual idea.

The image that's been working for me is putting a fancy blanket over a dog terd, still there, still a little noticeable.

Totally okay to let it dry out a little before you pick it up!

So, I've been using the opportunity this cancer time to clean my room, the banana peels (cancer) and the dirty socks (need for parental approval). I've recognized that whether I believe that the dirty socks came from a 16th century monk or my Uncle Roy, or myself, at some point I need to pick them up and decide if I want to keep them or not.

Inspiration spent I'm going to enjoy a rooftop beer with my brother, cheers!

Fawna

Radiation involved 20 sessions, 5 days per week of driving an hour and a half to Calgary for 5 minutes on the table in my mask. The technicians were quietly and efficiently heartfelt, I had a sense that they were perfectly at home in this dark space with its machines and order. For the most part I enjoyed the speed of driving myself, going to and from treatment directly. I had dozens of offers of drivers and there was an assumption that a driver would be needed. My fifteen year old Jake accompanied me for one session, we laughed as we read the words "It's a Party" hung as a 'Stampede' decoration in the radiation hallway, woohoo. I'm still regretting not getting a picture of my radiologist in his full Stampede gear. My radiologist, smiling as I write this, Dr. Balogh was the radiologist who saw me the first round. When I saw him this time I argued against radiation, he seemed confused and solid in his conviction that I needed radiation. I had the same argument with the Holy Spirit and heard "you will finish Western Medical Treatment." For me, radiation seems to bring out the greatest resistance. I said to Dr. Balogh, "Last time I had the hardest time with radiation, I was fine with chemo and did really bad with radiation." He answered "You HAD a stem-cell transplant, it wasn't my fault!" We laughed.

I read the resistance, discovering fears of burning and being trapped and just generalized bratty "I don't want to." On the brighter side, one of my friends had bought a monthly parking pass for me and I was grateful every day for the ease of getting in and out of the parking lot easily, small graces. Radiation came, and it went.

Chapter 27
Relaxing into Completion
8/7/12

Radiation ends
Modern medicine meets soul
Cancer - Zero, Fawna - Two
By: Dear Friend Kim Page Gluckie

Kim started a small "Haiku's for Fawna" group on Facebook shortly after my diagnosis.
AHHHHHH...first weekday in 4 weeks with no trip to the cancer centre. On Friday my parents drove me for my last radiation session, last time locked into the mask for a short but sometimes distressing 10 minutes. I had some moments of near panic in that mask and some moments of deep peace. One day I saw myself sitting in the audience watching the treatment like a show, sharing popcorn with the Holy Spirit. This last day the message was "you are not trapped," ahhhhh, felt it more than I heard it.
So on the final day I got off the table and the quiet east Indian tech said that laughing and smiling creates faster healing, I hugged my techs and BURST out crying on my way out. Another hug with the nurse and I sashayed out. The crying felt like relief, isn't it amazing how we can be 'holding it all together' and not even realize it?
SO, it feels like a time for reflection. A super easy going reflection though as opposed to a 'figure my life out' intensity that I felt 12 years ago after treatment. I feel like wearing flip flops (I'm wearing a 1970s muumuu that was my grandmas' as I write this) and just relax, inner tube floating vibe.

3 chemotherapies, 20 radiation sessions, mind watching all the way supported by energy work and a 'force of nature support' circle. Wow, as I write this I realize I'm exhaling, and exhaling...

The cancer has been a backdrop for RECEIVING (capitalized because it has been in such a big way), trusting and looking beyond appearances. A personal relationship with the Divine has been enhanced and oh so helpful.

Western treatment has a defined beginning and end, I've felt 'healed' (of the seeming cancer) for some time now, so while I'm of course glad that it's over there is also a sense of continuum, of the flow of life. I'm having a difficult time putting it into words; as I've gone through this I've realized how much investment we have put into the BIGNESS of cancer and equally cancer treatment, both alternative and western. This is a SERIOUS illness and requires IMMEDIATE and FULL attention. I'm laughing as I write this. In no way am I trying to minimize this experience, or anyone else's, okay, maybe I am, shit.

Would it be bad to minimize it, at least take a bit of the teeth out of it? The truth is, we all have crap-scary crap, all of us. Even if you mastered 'not suffering', there was a time that you HAD crap, its part of being here. We have taken all of these experiences and labelled them, we have quantified and qualified them, we have diverse horror scales (where cancer usually scores high) which may include divorce, bankruptcy, bad shoes, and so on.

I've shifted from believing that the suffering comes from outside in to believing that it is from the inside out. On a more positive note, the Peace is in there too.

As I move into the Peace, letting go of a 'personal' Fawna who 'things happen to', I hope you are feeling the compassion in this rather than a detachment, I'm moving more into Me, fun, joyful, free me and more into being able to know you, rather than judging who you are and where you are at.

Fun, Joyful, Free. Ahhh...not much more to say for now...exhaling.

Chapter 28
Undoing Emotions
8/23/12

Yesterday I posted on Facebook that I had been emotional for a couple of days now, this brought on a barrage of comments. The comments ranged from love to worry to 'YOU HAVE THE RIGHT TO BE EMOTIONAL" (all appreciated). What I was trying to relay is that I'm allowing the feeling rather than pushing it out, projecting it. Now I'm laughing at the word projecting, so much more technical and clean than blame, call it what it is, I'm resisting the temptation to blame. Even in sharing that message the power of it diminished.

So this morning I sit with this and with the funeral of a friend's 7 and 11 year old going on at this moment. I have to say I've felt this urge to flee from thoughts of this funeral, flee from other people's posts about how sad it is making them. Fleeing for me means fear; fight or flight. But what exactly am I afraid of. The fear of losing children is the obvious choice, I'm sure that it is partially true, but what is being unearthed is a fear of emotion.
As I sit quietly I see myself standing in a black dress waiting to be burned and vowing to show no emotion. This is just a side trip, an opportunity to once again 'blame' a feeling on a 'past life'. Not tempted I sit longer and ask the Holy Spirit to reinterpret this fear for me. I begin to see (re-member) that emotions, just like the physical perceptions, are a handy trick to reinforce the 'reality' of separation.

Let me explain, I saw how in my life I have avoided emotional circumstances and I hear these statements of fear, don't show your emotions, your emotions affect other people, if you are mad you will make other people mad, if you are sad you will make other people sad, etc., etc. I have even avoided being too happy, for fear of making other people sad by comparison. What power I have! I am in charge and in control of not only my emotions, but everyone who encounters me! A demigod for sure.

As with all the ego's ideas (and they are only ideas) emotions are judged as good and bad. It's good to feel sad, it's bad to feel sad, changing with the generations, keeping us stuck in doing, feeling like we have no control. The control comes at the level of choosing your 'puppet master', are you on the string of ego, tossed wildly about in the sea of duality (and by the way you believe you ARE the puppet master here). Or are you on the strings of a loving, eternally patient, all knowing power that only wills for your happiness?

The ego says, well, what would you have if you didn't have emotions, that would be boring 'no rain, no rainbows', selling it's cheap imitation happiness over pure Bliss. The funny thing is we buy it, we glorify it, glorifying our suffering and shared misery.

I could be wrong but I don't believe we need to do this, I am asking Holy Spirit to take control of my emotions, to repurpose, use what I had chosen to prove separation for communicating that we are one.

It is not hard to see that when it comes to emotions there is a grain of truth in this, we feel together, there is one mind and I think we are ready for some Bliss. I am making the switch from living outside in to living inside out, it feels like a process because I'm afraid and guilty, the purpose of sharing it here is not to convince anyone at all but to explain where I am at in this moment so that I can see it. The sharing over the past few months has been immensely helpful, so I will continue and I truly value your thoughts.

I am not suggesting that we should not be sad about children dying. I am suggesting looking at the sadness and what it brings up, what beliefs are hiding here so that we can move beyond feeling perpetually victimized.

Only Love to all those at the funeral today and the eternal spirits who brought us all together

Chapter 28
Listen
9/11/12

It's been a couple of weeks since I posted. We went away for family holiday for a week and now I'm 2 weeks into all three kids in school. Gus started graded one, Jakes in Grade 10 and Paige in Grade 9. I'm done treatment, officially on short term disability until October and have told my boss (brother) that I'm not coming back...
On Facebook I asked NOW WHAT- and I've been feeling NOW WHAT!
Talk about consistency, Spirit continues to echo the sentiment of my FAVORITE SONG, Simon and Garfunkels 59th St Bridge Song.
So did many of you.
Here is the list of Facebook friends suggestions:
* Golf
* Still until you hear what is next, in each moment
* Come to the studio and record something (Taylor Sound)
* Relax?!
* Tahiti/Bora Bora
* Now is the time for whatever is in your heart.
* Trip to Canmore for lunch with Aileen
* Sounds like a great time to just be!!!! Focus on the things you love, and time with those who are most important to you.
* Let everyone come and visit you to join in your "sitting in stillness" ... um ... but combining a bit of laughter, coffee and hugs!
* No thing....

* Embrace what you have accomplished and make plans for the next fifty or more years.
* How about secretarial for your dad .that will keep you busy (My Dad has a fantastic book in him, gestation greater than an elephant).
* How 'bout WRITE a book ... your story?!?!
* Just be... :)
* Take up the hula hoop
* Or competitive lawn darts
* Blue haired pole dancer, spice it up, keep in shape, have a giggle and trying something different!
* Sit and it will come to you.... xoxo It's all perfect :-)xo
* If anyone can feel comfortable waiting for the next step it's you Fawna - hope you enjoy this time of quiet and rest.
* Open space for possibilities - wonderful!
* Have Dusty dress up in just chaps and spurs....
* Come decorate a nursery!
* we should go to the ocean and figure it out:)
* You could let your hair down (Blue) and do whatever is your pleasure!
* Nice-do whatever makes you happy Fawna! You deserve it!
* Good luck leaving the Ranch!!!
 (MOM!)
* You are in luck Fawna we are looking for a pool girl!! Pay not great but the two piece outfit will match the awesome blue hair!!!
* Take care of you, Lady.....
* I figure, it is time to just be.

So let me tell you friends, 2 weeks of 'Being' is HARD! Great of course, great to see how tempted I am to reacquaint with past behaviours of busy-ness and being 'helpful'. How addicted I am to 'think' and 'plan' as opposed to just be.

I am following a couple of people on Facebook who are travelling the world guided by and trusting in Divine Providence. This means they are listening inside for where to go and when and trusting that funds, assistance and all needs will be met by God/Holy Spirit/The Universe. I have decided that I want to do that too but here in Longview, in my family. So I wake up and say, "Holy Spirit teach me, show me guide me and lead me in this day."

One day I was led to watch the movie Ever After, a Drew Barrymore Cinderella story. The Cinderella story is one of my favourites.

The title of this blog is listen, I am listening to all of these cues, the song, the suggestions, my inner guidance, my teacher is LIFE.

Here is how I am seeing the Cinderella story in the Fawna context.

I have spent my life working, self-righteously doing jobs, most in a a caretaker role and volunteering whenever possible (sometimes when not possible too)! Following the worlds ideal that you must effort, suffer, be nice, try harder- and be happy doing it.

I'm not complaining, or trying to paint a bad picture, it is very neutral, what I believed in at that time.

The evil stepmother and stepsisters are the ego, never good enough, always demanding, self-satisfying, and emphasizing having. The prince represents Holy Spirit, love at first site, providing everything without any expectations and requirements, only a choice, and it's my choice.

Cinderella (me) is the chooser, and I'm ready, I'm ready to put on my ball gown and put on the shoe that fits.

I know it doesn't seems like we have a choice, we hide that choice from ourselves, the choice, that is NOT in the world, but in the mind, a choice of Purpose, to love or fear, to connect or to separate. The choice to Love and Connect requires worthiness, not to be earned, but to be accepted. I have already been judged by the Prince - judged innocent.

So this is what I'm doing, taking 2 weeks to write one blog, living like the girl on the front of the Titanic, at the edge of life, focus on mystery rather than 'what I know is...', moment by moment, catching when I run back on the boat and start rearranging chairs-lol!

I'd love to hear what your favourite songs, favourite stories say to you, the mythology of you. I love you.

Chapter 29
Choosing to Live
9/27/12

Okay, I've decided what I'm going to do, I'm going to live. I made this decision several months ago, but as the circle of this cancer story comes to completion I am now sitting in contemplation of when I believe this healing began.

To close this circle I want to tell you the beginning. It feels as if I have been open in this journey but have left out a major plot element, I have hinted at it, mentioned it, but never given you the whole story.

It feels like time to share the healing vision.

I began to experience throat pain last May. It was diagnosed as strep throat off and on all summer and fall. I spent the fall working hard at two jobs, visiting medical and alternative treatment providers and thrashing around fighting my mind. I realize in hindsight that the medical professionals were mirroring my decision not to deal with what grew into a massive tumor filling my sinus cavity and literally coming out my nose. Until it was 'plain as the nose on my face' we were complicit in ignoring symptoms.

When my misery; a constant snotty nose, a snotty eye, a large mass filling the left nostril and an inability to nose breathe whatsoever, coupled with fatigue and weight loss came to a peak I surrendered my stubborn will to 'wish' it away and revisited my doctor. No begging was needed, she said, "OH MY GOD" when she looked up my nose. Now I waited to see a specialist, in this week the mass broke through the roof of my mouth, and growths showed up at my temple and on my neck, I called the doctor and said, "I need to see someone NOW."

We were on high speed from then. When I received the diagnosis of 'Recurring Non-Hodgkin's Lymphoma' one of my first actions was to contact a spiritual mentor and heart sister (a few of them actually).

Stacy Sulley is an energy practitioner, I quickly scheduled an appointment with her. When she called I shared what had been the primary message I had been given. I have been cultivating a relationship with Spirit for several years and now regularly get messages, if I remember to ask. The message I was getting was "Pull it out by the root." Stacy and I entered our session with this intention in mind.

This session was over the phone, I lay in my bed and put the speaker phone on my chest, closed the door and closed my eyes.

Stacy instructed me to breathe and we both became quiet, she repeated the intention to go to the root of the current issue. I dropped my awareness into my body, relaxing and allowing my consciousness to drift around the body. I don't really have a sense of the time, but sometime later I became aware of an intense irritation, and the sound of a baby crying. The plaintive sound of a newborn crying, the kind that puts most women on high alert. I sat with the crying, which I identified as me. I allowed that baby to cry and cry, witnessing. The story unfolded as follows, the baby was born (and I had a sense this was the first birth, not necessarily connected to my mother now) and the baby (I) was shocked and mad. "What the Hell is this?", "It's cold here," "I don't like it," "Get me out of here" - I probably don't have to explain it- but this is what I saw as 'the root' of the current issue.

I spent quite some time listening to the baby tell it's story, rant and rave and eventually it became quiet. I stayed with it. Suddenly there was a shift and the baby (I) was pulled back in, back to the womb. I experienced the birth experience again, this time warm, filled with love and understanding, aware. I was both watching and feeling this, and it gives me a big sigh even now.

I was thinking ahhh. There it is, that's it, and then bam, I was going back in again-this time there was no womb, it was just space. Vast openness, and the words were 'not expecting', 'no expectations', a sense of being.

I kind of came out of it there and said- OMG- Stacy did you see that? Did you feel that? She kind of chuckled and said, it's not done yet.

I brought my awareness back to this space and asked the babies questions "what is this," "what is the purpose of being here?" I asked again and again and there was a dawning understanding, a quiet voice (perhaps voices) patiently allowing me to ask until I was hearing and feeling, there is no question, there are no questions- and YOU are the answer. Repeatedly - YOU are the answer.

I feel vulnerable sharing this here, I hope you'll feel the message behind this, as I don't think I can put it clearly into words and it is almost like admitting something about yourself that you can hardly believe. I'm not sure why it feels so awkward, so embarrassing to express that I felt my Worth, my Power and inherent and everlasting 'Yes-ness'. I heard it over and over again, "there is no question, you are the answer."

I came out of the session, an hour and half later feeling a little shaken, but seriously happy to uncover a 'death wish'.

I could see how I always saw spirituality, goodness, relief, happiness out there, and had a general disdain for the world, the body, matter and materiality. I have been living a story of "Get me the hell out of here," lost in mind and spirit, ignoring and attacking the body whenever possible.

This session was on a Friday evening (good Friday :)), I saw my sister in Law on Friday and on Sunday and she and I both believed that the tumor was smaller and I was healthier on Sunday, on Monday I had my first chemo. By the next Friday there was no indication of the growth on my face, in my mouth, throat or temple.

I spent time praying on whether I needed to continue with Western Medicine, feeling strongly that I was healed. Thankfully the message was consistent, "you will complete your Western Medical treatment." From that time on I have, despite treatment, gotten healthier and healthier, weight consistent with few side effects.

Nouk Sanchez (www.undoing-the-ego.com) shared her learnings with me and they resonated deeply. Truly acknowledging the power of the Mind, the power of what you 'choose', often unconsciously coupled with her newfound realization that we can hear and feel this IN the body.

I came across this from Eckhart Tolle:

"Your physical body, which is form, reveals itself as essentially formless when you go deeper into it. It becomes a doorway into inner space. Although inner space has no form, it is intensely alive. That "empty space" is life in its fullness, the unmanifested Source out of which all manifestation flows. The traditional word for that Source is God." Eckart Tolle

So at that moment, and now, here in the reflective space of this beautiful autumn I am choosing life. For quite some time I had "Follow Your Bliss" on my Facebook, what I didn't know is that I had unconscious desires that were at odds with this, unconscious beliefs in a certain badness and a wish to destroy 'Fawna'. The weird thing is, I do want to destroy Fawna, the Fawna that thinks she is this little helpless piece of meat, relating to (and often afraid of) the other pieces of helpless meat. I want to re-member that 'Yes-ness', the part that was created from the Divine- and remains Divine.

So, choosing Life, which means choosing Love, which means choosing All, without separations.

That's what I'm going to do now.

Made in the USA
Charleston, SC
23 October 2016